RESET

Live Every Day Like It's a New Day

DALE HUMMEL

CORE.

Reset
Live Every Day Like It's a New Day
www.resetbook.org
www.dalehummel.com

Published by The Core Media Group, Inc.
P.O. Box 2037, Indian Trail, NC 28079
www.thecoremediagroup.com

Published in association with the literary agency of WordServe Literary Group, Ltd.,
www.wordserveliterary.com

Cover & Interior Design: Nadia Guy
Cover photo provided by Mrexentric/Pixabay, StockSnap/Pixabay.

ISBN 978-1-950465-53-8

Printed in the United States of America.

Table of Contents

To my wife Marcia, you are my best friend. No one has had a more loving and godly influence on my life than you. Thank you for never giving up on me, always praying for me, and walking alongside me through this journey called life.
I love you.

Introduction
Time for a Reset

I t happens far too frequently. I am busy at the computer, working on a project I've put off for too long, when all of a sudden, my internet connection fails. Now I'm even further behind. What a pain!

In frustration, I get out of my chair and head downstairs to the basement, where the modem is located. I follow the same routine: I disconnect all the cables and then wait for a minute before plugging them in again. Then I wait for the modem to reboot and pray the problem is fixed. Sometimes I have to repeat this process.

Why does this keep happening? I wonder. I decide to ask Google. I find an answer on lifehacker.com:

> There's no one universal cause...It could be that your internet provider changes your IP address often, and your router doesn't catch on. Maybe it's overheating, or maybe it's getting bogged down by too many connections at once....electronics are not built to constantly be running at all times, and power cycling helps with most issues. Like other electronics, one of the biggest reasons you may benefit from rebooting your modem is because when you leave your modem on for too long, it will tend to stop performing its best after a while....by unplugging the power cord from the back of the modem you are giving it the breather it needs....another reason is that when your modem's on all day,

every day, it is slowly desynchronizing from the internet service provider.[1]

I sit back, amazed. This answer, meant to help me understand my modem madness, actually helps explain what's been happening for years to my internal modem: my mind!

Here are the parallels I see between the issues with my computer modem and my mind:

- **"Your internet provider changes the IP address often, and your router doesn't catch on."** My life circumstances have and continue to change rapidly and unexpectedly, and my mind can't always keep up. Within the past year, I lost my mom unexpectedly, and my wife's best friend passed away, within a month of each other. While that was happening, I was trying to lead a large church, travel overseas to train Christian leaders, gear up for a multimillion-dollar campaign to raise funds to begin a fourth campus, establish eight to twelve thousand new churches in Asia, buy a theatre to house our third campus, and get ready for Thanksgiving and Christmas!
- **"Bogged down and overheating"**…otherwise known as burnout! I could feel my nerves sizzling. Several times over the past few years, I've felt like I was at a breaking point.
- **"Electronics are not built to constantly be running all the time…"** Neither is the human mind or body! Nevertheless, I continue to push myself, trying to prove otherwise.
- **"It [the modem] is slowly desynchronizing from the internet service provider."** All this combines to make me feel desynchronized from God, my provider. I have often asked, "Where are You, God?"
- **"By unplugging the power cord from the back of the modem, you are giving it the breather it needs…"** When that works with the router in my basement, I experience great relief, and life goes on. But when I have to repeat the process

---

1. Whitson Gordon, "Why Do I Have to Keep Resetting My Router, and How Can I Fix It?" Lifehacker, May 16, 2012, https://lifehacker.com/why-do-i-have-to-keep-resetting-my-router-and-how-can-5910788, accessed June 1, 2019.

several times, I grow angry and frustrated. *What's the matter with this piece of junk? Why isn't it rebooting like it usually does?*

What do you do when you can't reboot your mind?

That was the story of my life, and like every story, it has a beginning. As is true for most of us, my mental and emotional struggles began way back in childhood. I was born overseas to missionary parents, whom I believe did the best they could to raise a normal healthy boy. But even the best attempts sometimes fall short. Unfortunately, my folks were naïve to predators masked as friends and family.

At the age of seven, I was seduced and abused by a man who came to visit the mission station my folks had established in the remote jungle of Papua, New Guinea. I was left alone with this trusted person for an afternoon. He took advantage of my curious nature and led me into an evil web, where my soul would remain entangled for many years to come.

I suppose if it had been a one-time event, I might have gotten over it or packed it away into some deep, dark cave back in my subconscious. But soon afterward, our family went home on furlough, and I had to share a room with my older cousin, who picked up where the other man had left off. The abuse was chronic for the years we lived with and near him. It led to what I discovered was a network of abuse with other family members as well. I was passed around. Pandora's Box had been opened, and out of it a world of strange feelings, guilt, shame, and fear continually swarmed my mind.

If God has a plan for one's life, I'm convinced that Satan, the enemy of the soul, does as well. The abuse continued in my life well into my junior high years. I have wondered why I never told my parents or anyone else. The fact that I grew up in a religious environment at home and church, which made sex seem like something dirty, may have contributed to my silence. I did not want to disappoint my parents, pastor, or other spiritual leaders. I certainly did not want them to be angry with me.

By the time I entered puberty, I felt so guilty about the strange feelings and desires. I believed everything that had happened in my life was my fault, including the struggles my parents began having in their marriage. My dad was gone most weeks, starting a business in Canada, while my mom, brother, and I stayed in Michigan. I couldn't stand it when he came home on the weekends and they fought. I began to resent the emotional upheaval it created for me.

In the meantime, I was having a really hard time adapting to the tough blue-collar culture of the Midwest. We lived in a small town that had more bars than gas stations and where men and boys proved themselves with their fists. Unfortunately, I became a frequent punching bag. In junior high, I developed nervous tics similar to Tourette syndrome. I was in a cauldron of boiling emotions.

My religion did not help me. I grew up with a brand of theology that said you could lose your salvation when you sin. By the time I was a teenager, my soul had been thinly sliced by a thousand cuts of guilt, shame, and the fear that I was going to hell.

But I'm a survivor, and I always have been. I don't take credit for that drive, however. To this day, I believe that despite my circumstances, God was and is still in control. I realize that some people who go through what I've faced become angry at God. For some reason, I never felt that way. In fact, I felt just the opposite. I thought I was a very big disappointment to Him. I have never blamed God or turned my back on Him, though I did rebel, and I experienced the consequences of being exposed to the kinds of things that overtook my life at a young age. But God was faithful to me, even when those who represented Him were not. Eventually I would come to a truer understanding of His character and grace, which I share with you in this book.

Despite the odds that my life would turn out badly, I grew up to become a high-functioning dysfunctional adult. I somehow managed to keep all the pieces together enough to look "normal" on the outside, but within, my mental modem was melting down.

In 1995, an event occurred that I can only describe as an ambush on my life. I'll tell you more about that in the next chapter. It was a catalyst that propelled me toward finally discovering the secret to resetting my life mentally, emotionally, and spiritually, for the long term. On the way toward my freedom, I tried a lot of things.

My path was largely trial and error. I had appointments with great doctors, psychiatrists, psychologists, and counselors. I tried several different types of drugs to help me with my mental and emotional battles. While these medications work wonders for some people, the side effects were debilitating for me. Of course, I also tried praying, reading Scripture, and claiming various promises over my restless soul, but those didn't seem to work either.

But when my breakthrough happened, I suddenly saw how to think differently about what I was reading in God's Word. I discovered how to apply it in a way that began to change my life.

I'm not claiming I don't still have some mental and emotional struggles. But now I understand why I have them, which is half the battle. Knowing why has liberated me to reset my internal modem regularly and move on toward increasing victory rather than remaining stuck in a cycle of discouragement and lack of real change.

In *Reset: Live Every Day Like It's a New Day*, I hope to spare you the long road I had to travel and provide a direct route to your mental, emotional, and spiritual freedom. In the pages ahead, I describe how you can become free from the tyranny of past hurts and disappointments simply by changing your mind—which, in turn, will change your brain. I discuss sixteen aspects of resetting your mind as they relate to resetting your focus, identity, attitude, faith, and community. The Reset exercises provided within the chapters are designed to help you practice learning new ways to think and apply God's Word to your life. For your convenience, I have repeated all sixteen of the Resets, as well as all the Reset exercises, at the back of the book. Having them all in one place can facilitate your individual or group study.

Here are some of the benefits I've experienced and hope to pass on to you:

- Understanding the source of our mental, emotional, and spiritual battles (yes, we all have them!)
- Unpacking the truth of what God thinks about us in our struggles, regardless of whether we've brought them on ourselves or others have inflicted them on us
- Learning daily disciplines you can immediately apply that will reset and refresh your personal and relational life
- Learning how to grow through setbacks, which will occur!
- Understanding the importance of community in our healing

Now that you've read a bit about my story, what is your story? What's on your mind right now? I realize that no two stories are exactly alike, and I hope you have not experienced some of the things I have. But my guess is that your life has had some traumatic moments. Perhaps you're in a difficult place right now. Or maybe someone you love and care about is struggling. Is it your spouse? A son or daughter?

My wife was recently speaking to a professional counselor, who told her she is seeing a steady increase of children who are so mentally and emotionally stressed out they cannot cope with life. If you are a parent, the practices I teach you will enable you to help your children, too.

What about your religion? Do you feel it has failed you? What messages have spiritual leaders given you that have left you feeling "I'm not good enough for God" or "I've failed Him too often. He must be sick of me because I'm sick of myself!" Maybe that's a big part of the struggle people you care about are going through as well. I want you to hear a message from God that breathes hope and life, not judgment and condemnation.

Whatever your circumstances, I would like to invite you to join me on a journey that will lead to greater mental and emotional well-being. One of my favorite sayings, which I heard many years ago, simply states that our God is the "God of new day starts." I have found that to be true in my life. Are you ready for your new day start?

Let's begin!

Chapter 1
What's Wrong with Me?

In 1989, just after I graduated from seminary, my wife, two young children, and I packed and headed from Central Ohio, for Northern California. I had accepted an invitation to become the pastor of a church in the San Francisco Bay area.

Not long after arriving, we experienced our first earthquake. The Loma Prieta quake struck on October 17th. I remember it because I was standing in a field near Alameda Bay watching some high-schoolers from church play soccer. All of a sudden, the ground felt like a sieve that was being violently sifted back and forth. There was no wind, but the nearby palm trees were bending as if a gale force were blowing.

Despite the damage and loss of life caused by the quake, no one in our family or congregation was seriously hurt.

Since then, I've learned that earthquakes don't just happen. They are caused by a sudden release of stress along faults in the Earth's crust. In other words, down under the surface of the Earth, there's a whole lot of stress building up, waiting to be released. When it does, it shakes everything on top!

I would soon discover the same was true within me. The underbelly of my soul had been building up with stress for years. Cracks were beginning to show, but I did not read the signs until I was ambushed at dinner one night. But before I tell you about that episode, I want you to know that outwardly, I appeared to have it all together. If you had been a member sitting in my congregation, you would not have noticed anything was wrong. In fact, I think you would have thought everything was going really well. In many ways, it was.

The church was growing quickly. My wife and I had adopted a little boy. And somehow, I managed to find time for family, friends, and work-outs. But I was finding it increasingly difficult to cope, mentally and emotionally, with the life I was living. My mind would not shut off.

During that time, I was finding it difficult to sleep and would often lie awake at night with feelings of fear about everything. I had a deep feeling of being utterly alone, despite the fact I had a loving and caring wife and having recently adopted our son we now had three great kids and wonderful friends. It was so strange; I could not reconcile my thoughts and feelings, either mentally or spiritually.

Maybe you've had similar thoughts and feelings invade your soul. You don't want them to be there, but they show up unannounced. Are you plagued with ongoing feelings of guilt, shame, and fear? Do you wonder what's wrong with you? What are you losing sleep over? Believe me, I feel for you! If you don't get help, your pain will eventually get your attention in some unpleasant ways. I was about to find that out.

My *soul quake* happened at the family dinner table. Our family of five had sat down for dinner and engaged in normal conversation. That's when I felt the first tremor rising from the soles of my feet up through the trunk and limbs of my body. It was a heart-gripping fear. I shot up out of my chair and walked away from the table. My wife asked, "What's wrong?" I couldn't answer. I thought I was going to die! I walked into the narrow hallway of our home and slumped down against the wall. My heart was pounding, and I remember telling my wife, who had followed me, that I thought I might be having a heart attack. "Should I call someone?" she asked. I told her no, not unless I pass out or it gets worse. Eventually, the terrifying feeling subsided, and I was able to regroup.

What was that all about? I wondered. Over the next couple of months, I would be ambushed by more of these episodes. I kept asking myself and God, *Why? What am I doing wrong that You're allowing this to happen to me?*

Have you ever asked God questions like that? I knew I needed to get help.

I finally went to see my doctor. He listened to my symptoms and ordered a bunch of tests to determine if there was anything physically wrong. After several visits, he pulled up a chair in the examining room and said I was in great physical health. Apparently, my issues were all mental!

He advised me to go see someone in the mental health department. I refused. *I'm not a mental case*, I thought. So he suggested I take a class on dealing with stress. That felt better. It was just stress, and a class would solve all my issues. I went down to sign up for the class and found out there was a three-month waiting list!

I couldn't keep living the way I was living, so I finally made the decision to seek out a counselor I knew and felt I could trust.

I scheduled my first appointment with the therapist. I fretted over what I would do if I walked into the waiting room and saw a parishioner sitting there. I had a couple of lines prepared just in case: "Oh, hey, how are you? Yeah, I'm here to see Jacque. She's a good friend, and this was the best time to catch up. So I just made an appointment like I was a client…but I'm not." Or, "I'm here to see what it must be like for people when I recommend they see a counselor…" I found out later that she had graciously scheduled me when no one else would be in the waiting room.

My first session was the worst and best day of my life. It was the worst because I discovered I had to face my painful past. It was the best because I realized that until I dealt with the past, I could not overcome the present and move into a better future.

Are you prepared to be honest with your past, whatever it has been? Until you unpack, understand, and to some degree accept what has happened to you, you cannot leave it behind and move forward. In my case, there was someone in my past who desperately needed to be loved, someone I had neglected and left behind.

I thank God for Jacque. She was His hand of grace at a critical time in my life. God used her to reach back into my childhood and help me begin a healing journey that is still taking place, even as I write this. She helped me discover a young boy I had locked away in a closet. A child I blamed for all that was wrong in my life. I used to mock the idea that everyone has an inner child. I thought it was just psychobabble. But I was wrong! The little boy who needed loving and healing was me, and he was still hidden deep inside my adult life.

I suspect that when we adopted and demonstrated love toward the precious little baby boy who became our son, it triggered something deep in me. That little boy inside me, whom I had trapped in a closet of guilt and shame, was also crying out for love and attention, saying, *You've adopted and cared for Tim. Why can't you do the same for me?*

Jacque served as my first guide in helping me learn to love, understand, and forgive myself. In the coming chapters, I want to help you experience healing in your life, too. I want to show you how much you're loved and how important it is to learn to love yourself, no matter what! I want you to know and feel the tremendous value that God has placed on your life. But before we get to that, there are some issues you have to work through first—and the same was true for me.

Before I could truly love myself, I still had more to work through and understand before I could discover the secrets of enduring peace in my life. There was a lot of collateral damage from my past that needed sorting out. But it would take moving to Chicago to deal with that next chapter in my recovery.

In 2001, our family arrived in Naperville, Illinois, a western suburb of Chicago. My eldest son was already attending college in Iowa, so this move put us closer to him. More importantly, we felt it was God's call to help lead a church that was struggling. Despite the challenges the church was facing, the congregation had the courage and vision to move into the future and become a dynamic, leading church in the area. We grew from eight hundred to three thousand members and experienced some amazing years of ministry.

But under the surface, I was still mentally and emotionally struggling. I was constantly ruminating and fighting unwanted thoughts. I continued to struggle with bouts of self-hatred and unhealthy feelings of inadequacy. It was like my brain was stuck in a deep rut of hopelessness I could not escape. Despite experiencing a lot of healing regarding my past, I was suffering from a form of PTSD. My daughter, who has her graduate degree in the social sciences, recommended that I go see a therapist—again.

Once again, I fought the battle of shame. I'm a pastor, a professional caregiver, a man of God, an example to my congregation! What if people find out I'm seeing a shrink? It is much easier to tell someone you have a broken arm than to admit to them you're struggling with mental illness. People feel sorry for you and ask how you're doing when you tell them you broke your arm. But when they hear you're dealing with mental illness, they don't know what to say. They act like you're crazy! Well, aren't we all…just a little bit?

I found a Christian psychologist in the next town over. He was exactly the person I needed to take the next step in regaining better mental, emotional, and spiritual health. I had no doubt that God's hand was at work. After several sessions, Dr. Brad diagnosed me with obsessive compulsive disorder (OCD). Now I actually had a name and a diagnosis for what had been plaguing me most of my life. I was so happy! He even said I had a really serious case of it, which made me feel even better!

I know that may sound a bit odd—okay, really weird—but when you have suffered with something your whole life and have not been able to tell many people about it because you don't even understand it, but then finally you know what it is, it is very liberating!

So, what is OCD? There are many forms of the disorder. Mine has to do with obsessive and unwanted thoughts that kidnap my mind. Everyone experiences ruminating thoughts, but for approximately one out of fifty people, rumination is a serious problem.[1] I am one of those people. My OCD causes my brain to get stuck and ruminate on things that the other forty-nine people can easily dismiss. Given my past, I had gigabytes of stored thoughts, feelings, and experiences for my ruminating brain to obsess over.

In his book *Brain Lock*, Jeffrey Schwartz, MD, writes, "Together with many other brain scientists, our UCLA team believes that OCD is a brain disease, in essence a neurological problem. The thought does not go away because the brain is not working properly. So OCD is primarily a biological problem, tied to faulty chemical wiring in the brain. The form of OCD—the unrelenting intrusiveness and the fact that these thoughts keep reoccurring—is caused by a biochemical imbalance in the brain that may be genetically inherited."[2]

At this point, you may be wondering what kinds of things I obsess about. Here are some of them:

- I obsess over death. I cannot tell you how many times a day I think about dying. I don't want to die, but I keep getting

---

1. Mario Beauregard and Denyse O'Leary, *The Spiritual Brain: A Neuroscientist's Case for the Existence of the Soul* (HarperCollins, 2009), 127.
2. Jeffery M. Schwartz and Beverly Beyette, *Brain Lock: Free Yourself from Obsessive Compulsive Behavior* (Harper Perennial, 2009).

intrusive thoughts that I'm going to die at any moment.
- I obsess over the number six. It even bothers me to write it. It carries with it an evil connotation in my mind. Sounds ridiculous, doesn't it? I know, but it's true.
- I obsess over certain vulgar words I never use in my vocabulary but that invade my mind—usually when I'm tense, like before I preach!
- I obsess over demons, wondering if I'm possessed. I know I'm not…but maybe I am?
- This past Sunday, while I was preaching, I obsessed nonstop with the thought that I was doing it all for show. I was teaching with half my brain, while the other half was in a wrestling match with itself, trying to prove I was *not* doing it for show!
- I obsess over exercising enough: Did I get my full sixty minutes in?

That's enough for now, or I'll start obsessing about obsessing!

After discovering there is actually a name and diagnosis for what was going on in my brain, I wanted to know if there was any hope. Could I ever break free from the controlling intrusive thoughts that occupied my mind day and night? Could I ever find peace of mind?

In 2013, we moved to Minnesota. After twelve years of leading and serving a wonderful congregation at the Compass Church, God called us to a new opportunity in Eden Prairie, Minnesota. Through prayerful consideration, we accepted an invitation by Wooddale Church to join its leadership team. As the new senior pastor, it was my responsibility to help chart the future for this influential church. I was following a great pastor who, for thirty-five years, had led the Wooddale congregation to be a leading and transformative church in the Twin Cities and beyond. It was a privilege to follow in his footsteps and lead the church forward.

As we settled in, the pace of ministry increased—and unfortunately, so did my mental and emotional challenges. The combination of leadership stress, change, and adjusting to a new environment aggravated my OCD. I found myself increasingly plagued by self-doubt and the fear of failure. I was becoming irritable and angry, mostly with myself. The panic attacks I had first experienced in California eighteen years earlier were back again. I needed a breakthrough! I wondered if I was ever going to have a spiritual breakthrough and experience consistent peace in my life.

Finally, after years of mental and emotional suffering, I discovered an answer to my questions.

The answer came during a visit to the world-renowned Mayo Clinic. I was scheduled to get a physical. My doctor happened to also be a psychiatrist and had trained as a rabbi, so he took an interest in my life experiences. During my physical, he asked how the move was working out and how I was dealing with the stress that change always brings. I told him that dealing with stress was not a new challenge to me. I shared a bit about my past and told him about my OCD diagnosis. He suggested that I do a consult with someone he recommended in the mental health department of the clinic. *Here we go again*, I thought.

After meeting with the therapist for two hours, she recommended I take a new program that Mayo was offering called "Transform." She was optimistic and believed it could do what its name promises: transform my mental outlook on life. So I signed up. As they say, what did I have to lose?

Transform is a product of the research of a brilliant and compassionate Mayo physician, Dr. Amid Sood. Using his research and expertise, he blends together a scientific understanding of the brain and principles for retraining it to think in healthy ways.

The program began with an intensive two-day seminar aimed at helping us understand how the brain works and doesn't work. Over the next six months, our cohort did a monthly call with Dr. Sood. We had specific readings to do and journals to keep. During each conference call, Dr. Sood would briefly address the topic for the month and then lead us in a discussion. At the end of the six months, we gathered for a full-day retreat to give presentations and to share how Transform was changing our lives.

It was the first time in my life I felt like I was on the cusp of a mental, emotional, and spiritual breakthrough. It seemed strange that I had to go to a *medical* facility to have a *spiritual* awakening, but as you read on, you will see that the spiritual mind is profoundly affected by the biological brain. Until I understood the interplay between the mind and brain, all the prayer, Bible verses, and spiritual disciplines in the world would only lead to frustration!

Here are some of the major insights I gained from my Mayo experience.

Our Minds and Our Brains Work Against Us

The first idea that grabbed my attention was that my mind was colluding with my brain to work against me. I had fallen into a Jekyll and Hyde way of processing my thoughts. The words of Jesus in John 10:10 came to mind: "The thief's purpose is to steal and kill and destroy. My purpose is to give them a rich and satisfying life." I was dealing with two thieves: my mind and my brain!

In his book *The Mayo Clinic Guide to Stress-Free Living*, Dr. Sood puts it like this:

> The mind isn't a rational, pragmatic utilitarian. Rather, it's shortsighted, lacks self-control, is guided by rigid biases, jumps to premature conflicts, and frequently gets hijacked by impulses, infatuations, and fear. Although a phenomenal tool, the mind falls prey to distractions and the sway of emotions. The mind swims in a current of contradictory and competing predispositions. It wants to be happy, but forgets what will make it happy.[3]

I was so excited to read that! It was like he had studied my life and then wrote those words to describe me!

Does that description of the brain remind you of yours? You don't have to have OCD to have your thoughts hijacked by an unruly brain! Hopefully, you see why I wanted to know more about how the brain works.

Before I continue, let me tackle a big controversy in scientific circles. Are the brain and mind separate entities or one and the same? Materialists believe the mind is nothing more than the creation of the brain. In his book *The Spiritual Brain,* Dr. Mario Beauregard and Denyse O'Leary write, "In the materialist's view, our minds—soul, spirit, free will—are simply an illusion created by the electrical charges in the neurons of our brains. Nature is, as Oxford zoologist Richard Dawkins famously put it, a 'blind watchmaker.'"[4]

On the other hand, other scientific experts believe there is abundant evidence clearly pointing to the fact that the mind and brain are two separate entities. Researchers like Dr. Beauregard believe the mind is

---

3. Amit Sood, *The Mayo Clinic Guide to Stress-Free Living* (Boston: Da Capo Press, 2013), 24.
4. Beauregard and O'Leary, *The Spiritual Brain*, 1.

a nonmaterial reality that is very active *in* the brain but is not *of* the brain. Here is what he writes:

> The nonmaterialist approach to the human mind is a rich and vital tradition that accounts for the evidence much better than the currently stalled materialist one…non-materialist approaches to the mind result in practical benefits and treatments, as well as promising approaches to phenomena that materialist accounts cannot even address. Lastly…when spiritual experiences transform lives, the most reasonable explanation, and the one that best accounts for all the evidence, is that the people who have such experiences have actually contacted a reality outside themselves, a reality that has brought them closer to the real nature of the universe.[5]

As evidence of the mind's influence on the brain, Dr. Beauregard cites research by Dr. Jeffrey Schwartz:

> Jeffrey Schwartz, a nonmaterialist UCLA neuropsychiatrist, treats obsessive-compulsive disorder—a neuropsychiatric disease marked by distressing, intrusive, and unwanted thoughts—by getting patients to reprogram their brains. Their minds change their brains.[6]

Here's my very nonscientific view of things. Materialists see the brain like a movie projector, and the mind is the movie it produces on the screen. As a nonmaterialist, I believe the mind is the producer who loads the movie into the projector of the brain, which then projects the outcome on the screen. The problem, as you will see, is that the projector is broken, and the producer is fallible!

That leads me to my next two insights, which explain how the brain is broken and how it can be reprogrammed. (In chapter 2, we will see how the *mind* is broken and how to begin renewing it to produce a healthy life. A healthy mind leads to a healthy brain.)

---

5. Kirk A. Bingaman, *The Power of Neuroplasticity for Pastoral and Spiritual Care* (Lanham, Maryland: Lexington Books, 2014), 17.
6. Wolf-Ekkehard Lönnig, *Die Affäre Max Planck*, 49.

The Two Modes of the Human Brain: Focus and Default

The second major insight I discovered was that the brain has two modes: a focus mode and a default mode.[7] In the focus mode, we give our full attention to someone or something. We forget about ourselves and zero in on a project, a person, a game—whatever has captured our attention. When the mind is in focus mode, it doesn't see or think about anything else except what it is focused on.

In his book *12 Rules for Life: An Antidote to Chaos*, Dr. Jordan B. Peterson describes an experiment performed by Dr. Dan Simons:[8]

> Dr. Simons produced a video of two teams of three people. One team was wearing white shirts, the other, black...Each team had its own ball, which they bounced or threw to their other team members, as they moved and feinted in the small space in front of the elevators where the game was filmed. Once Dan had his video, he showed it to his study participants. He asked each of them to count the number of times the white shirts threw the ball back and forth to one another. After a few minutes, his subjects were asked to report the number of passes. Most answered "15." That was the correct answer. Most felt pretty good about that. Ha! They passed the test! But then Dr. Simons asked, "Did you see the gorilla?
>
> Was this a joke? What gorilla?

When the students watched the video again, they didn't count the passes of the ball. Instead, they looked for the gorilla—and there he was! A man dressed in a full gorilla costume appeared right in the middle of the game. He pounded his chest and acted like a beast, but because the participants had been focused on counting the passes, they missed it.

If you want to try this out on some friends, you can find the video on YouTube by searching for "selective attention test"—but don't tell them about the gorilla!

Apply that concept to the things you focus on. I'm not talking so much about the *outward* tasks we focus on to complete, but all the

---

7. Sood, *The Mayo Clinic Guide to Stress-Free Living*, 12.
8. Peterson, *12 Rules for Life*, 96–97.

internal things our minds get stuck on. For example, have you ever had the experience of being so deep in thought while you were driving that you somehow arrived at your destination but had no recall of how you got there?

You don't know where you left your keys? What were you thinking about when you put them down? You don't have Alzheimer's; you were simply focused on something more important than remembering where you put your keys. That's the *focus mode*.

Now let's look at the brain's *dominant mode*—the default mode. When we are in default mode, we are unfocused. Our thoughts wander. Where do they wander to? They usually drift toward the past or the future. It is very difficult to keep them in the present.

To make matters worse, when our thoughts wander to the past, they do not gravitate toward good memories. Earlier today, my mind wandered back seven months ago, when my mother passed away. She died a particularly painful death and was in excruciating pain right up to the end. It is easy for me to get fixated on the grimacing pain expressed on her face, my decision to put her in hospice, and telling her she could not go home. I cry as I think about her passing.

Did you notice that when my thinking wandered to my mom, it focused on the negative?

But what about all the great memories? My mom was a faithful and godly woman whom the Lord used greatly in her missionary days. My mom was a devout woman of prayer. She was loving and kind, and she helped so many people as a nurse. She really made a difference in this life! But my mind wants to drift to the sad things, the bad things, when I could be focusing on all the *good* things about her life.

Our minds, in many ways, remind me of vultures soaring and wandering the sky, looking for dead and rotting meat to swoop down and consume. In the same way, our minds ruminate over negative memories; they linger over regrets, hurts, and pain. Similarly, when the mind thinks about the future, it gravitates toward what may go wrong and ponders possible negative outcomes.

How about your mind? Where did it wander today? Did it focus on the good and positive things, or did it pull an Eeyore on you? Remember the pessimistic little donkey in the Winnie the Pooh stories? All he could see was what was wrong:[9]

> Eeyore, the old grey Donkey, stood by the side of the stream, and looked at himself in the water.
>
> "Pathetic," he said. "That's what it is. Pathetic."
>
> He turned and walked slowly down the stream for twenty yards, splashed across it, and walked slowly back on the other side. Then he looked at himself in the water again.
>
> "As I thought," he said. "No better from *this* side. But nobody minds. Nobody cares. Pathetic, that's what it is."
>
> There was a crackling noise in the bracken behind him, and out came Pooh.
>
> "Good morning, Eeyore," said Pooh.
>
> "Good morning, Pooh Bear," said Eeyore gloomily. "If it *is* a good morning," he said. "Which I doubt," said he.
>
> "Why, what's the matter?"
>
> "Nothing, Pooh Bear, nothing. We can't all, and some of us don't. That's all there is to it."
>
> "Can't all *what*?" said Pooh, rubbing his nose.
>
> "Gaiety. Song-and-dance. Here we go round the mulberry bush...I'm not complaining, but There It Is."

Sound familiar? How do you see yourself? How do you feel about yourself? Does your mind wander to the good things in your life or to the negative things?

In describing the mind's propensity to gravitate toward negative things, Dr. Sood uses the term "open files." In their book *Willpower: Rediscovering the Greatest Human Strength*, Roy F. Baumeister and John Tierney estimate that an average person's bucket list includes 150 undone tasks (open files).[10] How many open files do you have? This concept reminds me of my desk at work. By all appearances, it looks fairly neat, but when you open the drawers, there's chaos hidden just beneath the surface.

I don't know about you, but every night when I lay my head on my pillow to go to sleep, my mind opens the drawers of unfinished tasks

9. A. A. Milne, *The World of Pooh* (Boston: E. P. Dutton, 2010), 70–71.
10. Sood, *The Mayo Clinic Guide to Stress-Free Living*, xiii.

and accumulated unresolved worries and ruminates on what still needs to get done! Does yours?

No wonder more than 60 million Americans experience sleep deprivation![11]

Why does the mind wander toward all things negative? Dr. Sood believes a person's mind is like a sentry standing guard over any perceived hazards that could affect his or her life, or the lives of those one feels responsible for. In other words, our minds are always vigilant for any kind of danger, perceived or imagined.[12]

But it isn't just *threats* that occupy our minds. Consider the endless *desires* that also attract our attention. The undisciplined mind is easily taken in by thoughts of pleasure and short-term gratification. The problem with ruminating over our desires is that it leaves the mind even more restless. One becomes addicted to seeking the next novel thrill. Remember what it was like when you were a kid: What was that toy or that electronic gadget you just had to have, and if you had it, you would never ever ask for anything else, ever again? *Please! Please! Please!* If you got it, how soon did you get sick of it and require the newer and better version?

Human desires never seem to be satisfied, do they? We struggle to stop, say no, or make disciplined choices because we allow our cravings to control our lives. In a world that urges us to live in the left lane, no wonder our minds become impulsive and jittery, moving from one thing to another. The result is weariness, regret, and worry.

Neuroplasticity

Now that I was beginning to understand my dysfunctional mind and brain, how could I change them? We will talk about the *mind* in the next chapter. Let's focus here on the *brain*. The change can be summed up in one word: *neuroplasticity*! It's now one of my most favorite words. What is it?

Dr. Mario Beauregard writes that a central dogma of early neuroscience was that the neurons of the adult brain do not change. However, modern neuroscience now recognizes that the brain can reorganize

---

11. "Can't Sleep? Neither Can 60 Million Other Americans," *Talk of the Nation*, NPR, May 20, 2008, https://www.npr.org/templates/story/story.php?storyId=90638364?storyId=90638364.
12. Sood, *The Mayo Clinic Guide to Stress-Free Living*, location 389.

throughout life, not only in early childhood. This ability to reorganize is called "neuroplasticity." Our brains rewire to create new connections, set out on new paths, and assume new roles.[13] Dr. Sood describes the brain's ability to change this way: "Your brain remodels each time you acquire a new idea. Your thoughts re-create your brain or, more precisely, orchestrate how nerve cells grow and connect with each other."[14]

In other words, you and I can change our brains! If we can combine a changed brain with a changed mind, perhaps the possibilities for peace and joy are within reach!

Dr. Sood teaches that rewiring the brain requires a discipline of *attention training*, which involves learning to find joy and novelty by focusing the brain in the present moment. For example, as I write this, we have thunderstorms moving through the area. The clouds are heavy, gray, and foreboding. When I was a child, I was deathly afraid of thunderstorms. I associate negative memories with them and the fear that they might spawn tornadoes.

Dr. Sood calls the second discipline *refining interpretations*,[15] which is learning to apply higher principles to what one is attending to. As we learn to train our attention on the present moment, we interpret it according to a higher virtue. Dr. Sood focuses on five of these virtues: gratitude, compassion, acceptance, higher meaning, and forgiveness.[16]

For example, as I look at the stormy sky, I *choose* to notice the beauty and uniqueness of the cloud patterns. They are remarkable and remind me of God's power and artistry in creation. I am thankful that, as threatening as the sky may seem, there is beauty in all that power.

My attitude toward the sky and storm have changed. I am far less threatened and now view the sky as a canvas. I'm exploring what the Artist is trying to portray.

Sounds too simple, doesn't it? I mean, if it's that easy, why do we have such trouble changing our minds?

Jesus once asked a lame man a very curious question. The man was lying next to a pool of water. Any time the water was disturbed, it was believed that the disturbance was created by an angel and the first person in the water was healed. In John 5:10, Jesus asks the man

---

13. Beauregard and O'Leary, *The Spiritual Brain*, 103.
14. Sood, *The Mayo Clinic Guide to Stress-Free Living*, 10.
15. Ibid., xiii.
16. Ibid., xix.

straight out, "Do you want to be healed?"

That may seem like a very strange question to ask someone who is lame. Of course he wants to be healed, doesn't he? Not everyone does. I've met people who talk about wanting to be healed all the time, but they are unwilling to do the hard work to get better. When you get used to being sick, you actually fear getting well! *What will life be like if I'm whole and sound? Who will take care of me then? What will be expected of me?* We complain a lot about things that we don't honestly want to change.

It's like a golfer who has developed a bad swing. If you get in the habit of swinging at the ball poorly, you can almost guarantee you'll hit the ball poorly each time. But it is so hard to change your swing when the poor swing has been your default for years. It just feels right, even though it's wrong!

The same thing is true with our thoughts. We get used to thinking poorly, and to think in a new and different way feels unnatural. Your brain actually fights it because you have literally created grooves in your gray matter, and it is hard to get out of the ruts! The only way to overcome this is to learn to *ignore* what your brain is telling you. For a person like me who has OCD, that is a crucial strategy.

For example, when I'm getting ready to speak and a vulgar string of words crosses my mind, my initial reaction is to fight them by getting down on myself and wondering how this is happening after everything I've done to be spiritually fit. *Why now? Why me?* I go into confession mode and guilt mode and spiral into spiritual defeat. The more I wrestle with it, the harder it slams me to the mat.

What's the key to victory? How do I shut these thoughts down? I ignore them. I simply act as if I never had the thoughts in the first place. I've learned to say, as Dr. Schwartz teaches in *Brain Lock*, "It's not me, it's OCD." Instead of ruminating, I redirect my thoughts toward something wholesome and positive. I shun guilt and shame, and slowly my brain gives up, and I can think soundly!

But that's only half the battle. It is one thing to be able to retrain your *brain*. What about your *mind*? After all, it's your mind that wore the wrong grooves into your brain! Change your mind, and you will change your brain. In the next chapter, you'll discover how to change your mind. And you will begin to see that nothing is wrong with you—we are hardwired to think the way we do, and we can work around that!

Chapter 2
What's *Really* Wrong with Me?

M y wife and I recently applied for long-term care insurance. Watching our aging parents with their challenges has made us realize that we need to proactively think about minimizing our future financial risks.

We filled out all the paperwork, sent in the information, and waited for the underwriter's approval. Several weeks later, I received a phone call from our agent. He said, "Well, Dale, I have the proverbial good news and bad news!"

My wife is a skydiver with nearly a thousand jumps under canopy, so I assumed that the bad news had to do with insuring her. I figured they were either going to deny her coverage or ask for some special exclusion in case any disability was related to skydiving. Boy, was I shocked when he said, "Marcia passed with flying colors." All we had to do was sign some papers and send the check!

"Dale," he said. "They've denied you coverage."

"Why?" I asked.

He said because of legal reasons, they could not tell him. All he knew was that it had something to do with my medical records. It didn't take me long to figure it out. Just one little line in my documentation said I had been diagnosed with OCD and related anxiety. The underwriter told me that it was too high a risk for their company. It didn't matter that tests showed my blood, heart, and other important systems to be in excellent shape. They didn't want to insure someone with mental illness. Of course they didn't say it that way, but it was certainly implied!

In the previous chapter, we talked about what was "wrong" with us—our brain's tendency to focus on the negative. But this tendency is merely a symptom of a deeper problem. In this chapter, we're going to talk about the true cause of the problem.

According to The National Institute of Mental Health, one in five Americans has a diagnosable mental disorder, which equates to roughly 43 million people.[1] The National Alliance on Mental Illness says, "A mental illness is a condition that affects a person's thinking, feeling or mood. Such conditions may affect someone's ability to relate to others and function each day."[2]

If one takes that definition literally, I think it's a fair statement to say that everyone is a bit mentally off, don't you? Has anyone accused you of being a bit moody? Have you been guilty of some stinking thinking lately?

Seriously, don't we all struggle with our thinking and feelings, even more than we might want to admit? Why? What's behind all the mental and emotional battles we face? What's *really* wrong with us? I believe it can all be traced to one terrible day!

Before we visit the most terrible day in history, let's start with, "In the beginning…" Genesis 1:26–27 tells us, "Then God said, 'Let us make human beings in our image, to be like us…' So God created human beings in his own image. In the image of God he created them; male and female he created them." We also learn, in Genesis 2:7, how God created man: "Then the Lord God formed the man from the dust of the ground. He breathed the breath of life into the man's nostrils, and the man became a living person."

By the way, if you don't necessarily hold to a biblical worldview of how life began, I hope you will still consider what the Scriptures say about the human condition. It makes so much sense. As the rest of this book unfolds, you will see how the words and actions of the Creator can be the catalyst for mental and emotional healing in one's life.

In my spiritual journey I have often struggled with my own doubts

1. Thomas Insel, "Post by Former NIMH Director Thomas Insel: Mental Health Awareness Month By the Numbers," National Institutes of Health, https://www.nimh.nih.gov/about/director/thomas-insel/blog/2015/mentalhealth-awareness-month-by-the-numbers.shtml.
2. "Mental Health Conditions," National Alliance on Mental Illness, https://www.nami.org/Learn-More/Mental-Health-Conditions, accessed March 23, 2021.

and skepticism. However, one of the greatest proofs of God's reality occurs when I apply the truths of Scripture to my circumstances. In the chapters ahead, you'll have the opportunity to test-drive some of these principles and determine for yourself if they work.

Back to the genesis of all things.

When God created the human race, He endowed the first two living beings with many unique attributes that distinguished them from all other creatures. One of those unique attributes was the soul, or the immaterial part of one's life that relates to and is influenced by God. It is often defined as including the heart, mind, will, and emotions.

As part of the soul, let's take a deeper look at how the mind works and our ability to think. In his book *Renovation of the Heart*, the late philosopher Dallas Willard, PhD, describes *thoughts* as "all of the ways we are conscious of things."[3] According to an article in the *Huffington Post*, the average person has between fifty to seventy thousand thoughts a day! That's thirty-five to forty-eight thoughts per minute![4] Even while I've been trying to write these last few paragraphs, my mind has been bombarded with other competing thoughts, such as these:

- The advice I gave a staff member who is trying to navigate a serious relational issue. Did I give him good guidance? Should I risk getting involved?
- My grandkids from Vienna, Austria, are visiting. We're supposed to take them to an amusement park. The weather is not looking good on the day we're scheduled to go; do I make alternative plans?
- It's summer—why is the weather so cool, windy, and wet? Oh, I forgot, I live in Minnesota!
- Should I go biking tomorrow, or will it be too cold?
- Look at the squirrel! (Not really, but I have also been diagnosed with ADHD.)

What about you?

---

3. Dallas Willard, *Renovation of the Heart: Putting on the Character of Christ* (Colorado Springs: NavPress, Inc., 2002), 96.
4. Bruce Davis, PhD, "'There are 50,000 Thoughts Standing Between You and Your Partner Every Day!" *Huffington Post*, May 23, 2013, https://www.huffpost.com/entry/healthy-relationships_b_3307916.

I invite you to stop and take a few minutes to collect some of the thoughts that have been bouncing around in your mind. Besides the thoughts you're conscious of, there are all kinds of other considerations at your subconscious level!

How do we come up with these thoughts? According to Willard, human thinking includes four main components: ideas, images, information, and our ability to think—and "the two most powerful ones are ideas and images."[5]

Ideas are the assumptions we form with our thoughts.

My wife recently made us a fortieth wedding anniversary cake. She mixed several different ingredients together, baked the mixture, made her own special frosting, and slathered it over the chocolate cake—with sprinkles to boot! She served it up warm with vanilla bean ice cream. It was amazing!

So, what does a cake have to do with *thoughts* and ideas? The thoughts are the many ingredients, and the *idea* is the cake. In other words, behind every idea is a group of thoughts.

What ideas have been floating around in your mind recently? Can you identify the thoughts that went into forming the ideas?

Images are the expressions of one's thoughts and ideas into pictures or symbols. These images may be concrete or imagined. In either case, they stir up strong emotions. I mentioned that two of my grandsons are visiting. They found albums filled with their baby pictures. As they paged through the books, I found myself getting very sentimental. Just the images of them in their cribs, sitting up for the first time, crawling, standing, and walking, all bring back the best of memories and a broad smile to my face.

After my mother passed last year, my wife put together a memory box for me, and on the lid she put a picture of my mom when she was a young woman. I haven't been able to open it yet because when I see her image on that box and think of some of the treasures in it, my heart aches. The last words my mom spoke to me in hospice were, "Please get me out." I had to restrain her and say no. We never spoke again.

Images are powerful, aren't they? What are some of the visual images that move you?

---

5. Dallas Willard, *Renovation of the Heart: Putting on the Character of Christ* (Colorado Springs: NavPress, Inc., 2002), 96.

What stimulated Adam and Eve's ideas and images? I believe it was the Creator, God, who informed their beings. He was the original source of all their *information*, which is Willard's third main component of thoughts. God gave them understanding about who they were and the meaning behind the environment He created for them to tend to. Most importantly, God gave them a deep sense of their worth and value to Him and to each other.

Let me pause here and say how eager I am for you, in the chapters that follow, to discover how many good things God thinks about you! When you begin to actualize His thoughts toward you and others, it will be life changing!

But first, we need to explore what went wrong. How did the human mind become corrupted?

In Genesis, we discover that God placed the man and woman in a paradise called the Garden of Eden. They were free to eat the fruit from any of the trees in the garden—except a tree called the Tree of the Knowledge of Good and Evil. God warned Adam and Eve that taking that fruit would spiral them toward their eventual death. Not only would their choice affect them; it would also infect the souls of all their posterity.

Whatever you think about that tree, whether literal or symbolic, the point is that God was warning the couple to use the gift of choice to choose life. God wanted them to trust His Word about what was best for them and the world He created for them to manage.

And then came a terrible day:

"The serpent was the shrewdest of all the wild animals the Lord God had made. One day he asked the woman, 'Did God really say you must not eat the fruit from any of the trees in the garden?'
'Of course we may eat fruit from the trees in the garden,' the woman replied. 'It's only the fruit from the tree in the middle of the garden that we are not allowed to eat. God said, 'You must not eat it or even touch it; if you do, you will die.'
'You won't die!' the serpent replied to the woman. 'God knows that your eyes will be opened as soon as you eat it, and you will be like God, knowing both good and evil.'
The woman was convinced. She saw that the tree was beautiful and its fruit looked delicious, and she wanted the wisdom it would

give her. So she took some of the fruit and ate it. Then she gave some to her husband, who was with her, and he ate it, too. At that moment their eyes were opened, and they suddenly felt shame at their nakedness. So they sewed fig leaves together to cover themselves."

—Genesis 3:1–7

Did you notice how the serpent approached the couple? Through their *minds*! He suggested to them the *thought* that God could not be trusted. He used his crafty question to compel them to judge the motives of the Creator. Then he gave them new *information*: they wouldn't actually die upon eating the fruit. The evil one planted the *idea* that they could be their own gods by taking what God was holding back from them. Suddenly, the fruit of the tree became an alluring *image* of power and the pathway to self-existence!

They could either trust God was speaking the truth to them or believe the lie that they could be their own source of truth.

I don't need to tell you the choice they made because we live with the consequences of it every day! Adam and Eve fell from being God-centered to being completely self-centered. One of the proofs of the fallout from the Garden is our own personal experience. I'll admit it: I'm like my first parents, Adam and Eve—very self-centered! Are you? Look at social media, watch the news, listen to conversations; we're all into ourselves and fearful of anyone who might threaten our sense of security. Evolutionists call it *survival of the fittest*; the Bible calls it *sin*.

What is sin? The simplest definition is "to miss the mark." Think of someone standing in front of a bull's-eye, his bow drawn, aiming his arrow to the center of the bull's-eye on the wall. He is aiming for the center of the bull's-eye, but when he lets go, the arrow misses the mark by a wide margin—misses wide of the target—it doesn't even hit the target.

Sin is missing wide of the target, which is truth! Instead of beginning with information from God and interpreting life and relationships through the lens of His Word, we begin with ourselves (as the evil one told Eve, "You will be like God") and become the judge of what's true. We look to ourselves and everything else as the source of truth. The irony is that everything else becomes the judge of us.

The result is that our views are never truly our own. Everything we believe about ourselves and our environment is influenced by the information, ideas, and images of others. Like a computer attacked by a virus, our minds are easily infected by wrong thinking.

For example, when my parents returned from the mission field, we moved to a tough blue-collar town in central Michigan. My mom homeschooled me the first few years, and then my parents plopped me into public school in the fifth grade. I say "plopped" because it felt like they just clumsily dropped me into the culture, assuming I was prepared to handle it—but I was not!

I was already being sexually abused at that point, and now I faced a different kind of cruelty: bullying. I was a misfit. Even though I had spent my early childhood living among primitive natives in Papua, New Guinea, nothing prepared me for how savage other kids could be.

Over the next five years, I came to believe that I was stupid, fat, ugly, and quite worthless. Why? Because that's what I heard nearly every day. I heard it from my peers and even from some teachers. One of those teachers was my ninth-grade physical education instructor. He was a towering athletic figure whose size and strength reminded me of what Goliath must have been to David, except I was no David!

I quickly realized that he didn't have patience with clumsy kids like me. There were a few of us in class who became the victims of his chronic insults. I guess he thought he could motivate us by shaming.

Whoever said, "Names will never hurt me" was a liar. I'll never forget the teacher's favorite line whenever I missed a basket or finished last in a drill: "Hummel, if you were my dog, I'd shave your butt and make you walk backwards!" Everyone got a big laugh out of it. But I've never forgotten it.

Here's my point. If you hear the wrong information long enough, you eventually begin to believe it. While it is true that many of us who suffer from mental illness can blame it on genetics or chemical imbalances, I believe the predominant struggle we have, mentally and emotionally, is that we've come to believe the wrong information. We believe lies that masquerade as truth.

Think about it! What feeds racism, terrorism, greed, jealousy, social injustice, and so many other ills in our culture? Lies we believe are the truth!

What are some of the lies that have created the wrong thoughts, ideas, and images you have about yourself? What are your kids hearing about themselves? And just as important, what have you come to believe that you may be incorrectly imposing on others?

Are you ready to hear the truth about yourself and the world? Do you want to start thinking differently? You can, and you will. For just as there was one terrible day that ruined the world, you'll discover in the next chapter one magnificent day that began a change that can transform your world.

To fully experience the transformation of the Christian life, you do have to know the truth, but right information isn't enough! I can tell you from experience that you can pray, study the Bible, get a degree in theology, listen to sermons, read books, shame yourself, and try to root out every secret sin that you believe may be keeping you from living out the freedom of your Imago Dei (the image of God) and *still* not experience the freedom that knowing Christ promises.

What's missing? You haven't changed the way you think, which is Willard's fourth component of thinking. I believe that the words of the apostle Paul to Christ followers in Rome are powerful reminders that there's a very practical side to the spiritual: "Let God transform you into a new person by changing the way you think. Then you will learn to know God's will for you, which is good and pleasing and perfect" (Rom. 12:2b).

That verse is worth writing in your journal and memorizing with your mind.

Might the idea of neuroplasticity be hidden in Paul's words?

Here is where cutting-edge science meets ancient wisdom. It is true that lasting transformation requires building new neural pathways for the truth to begin altering how you're used to thinking, feeling, and behaving.

Think of it this way. I remember when personal computers first came out. It was amazing! But as new PCs were built and software was written, what was once amazing became frustrating and antiquated. Can you imagine trying to surf the internet or run today's applications on the first generation of personal computers? You'd pull your hair out in frustration. Why? Incompatibility! You cannot run the new on the old! Jesus once said, "And no one puts new wine into old wineskins. For the old skins would burst from the pressure, spilling the wine and ruining the skins. New wine is stored in new wineskins so that both are preserved" (Matt. 9:17).

The same is true with your brain. You cannot run the new way of thinking on the old operating system! In other words, you cannot expect your old default method of thinking to be able to accommodate the new. It will just lead to frustration, and you will continuously slip back into the old, repeated patterns.

You have to abandon the old pathways and create new ones. That's what the remainder of this book is about.

I want to share with you not only the wonderful truth about who you are, but how you can change your thinking to create new wineskins (new neural pathways) to fully receive the new wine of key Christian teachings—and begin living out the Imago Dei more fully.

To do this, I'm going to ask you to do some visioning and practical exercises that may take you out of your comfort (default) zone. But until you leave what you're used to, you cannot embrace what God has waiting for you.

As Christians, we have spiritual truths sitting right in front of us, but our habits of thinking have worn grooves into our brains that keep us believing lies. We read the truth in the Bible, pray for God to change us, and then get angry at God because we don't change.

But as Romans 12:2 shows us, if we are to change, there are things we also have to do on a psychological and neurological level. Getting angry at God for not changing us is like driving by the gym and getting angry at the trainer inside because we aren't losing weight. How can we lose weight if we never do the work?

The goal of this book is to help you do the work of transformation by changing the way you think—by doing a life-changing *reset*. In fact, I'd like you to think of me as your trainer. I've spent a lot of time working out at local gyms and health clubs. On occasion, I've had a trainer work with me to help me maximize my results. Having someone spend some time training me has always helped me achieve or improve my physical goals.

Just as you might do exercises on the equipment at the gym to strengthen and condition your muscles, in our sessions, you're going to be doing your Reset exercises, which involve your whole self and are repeated over time, to strengthen and condition your soul, which includes your mind. Your equipment will consist of a Bible, a pen, and a journal.

First, let's talk about Bibles. If you're unfamiliar with the Scriptures or not sure which version to use, two of my favorite translations are the New Living Translation and the English Standard Version. You can also purchase and download apps that will give you multiple versions to use. Many people have found the app YouVersion (youversion.com) easy to use.

Now, let's talk about journaling. You may be thinking, "I hate journaling. It doesn't work for me!" Well, give it one more try—maybe this time, it will work! If you were trying to increase the size of your biceps but hated doing curls and then found out that trying a new exercise with the same curling bar would promise you some big guns, would you try it?

By the way, if you think I am just talking to men, you're wrong! My wife, who is petite and works out three times a week at the gym, is ripped! If you want to get spiritually ripped, try journaling!

Your Bible and journal will become very important parts of your healing and transformation. I will be encouraging you to write down what you hear God saying to you. Your journal will also be a place to record important principles and personal reflections, as well as how God is changing your life. As you learn and grow, you will discover, again, that nothing is wrong with you! God made you in His perfect image. Yes, we are all human, and therefore not perfect, but we can learn to live every day like it's a new day by walking in His Word and following His guidance for dealing with everyday frustrations and fears.

As we use the principles of neuroplasticity to change our minds the way God intended, my hope is that we can not only change our thinking, but change our emotions, change our behavior, and maybe even create a whole new way of living together in service to the world.

Chapter 3
Reset Focus

I've had a few significant and mysterious moments in my life, which I can only explain as heaven breaking in on Earth.

One of those experiences happened when I was about eight years old. My family had been back from the mission field for about a year. After living with other family members and renting a house, we moved to my grandfather's farm in Harrow, Canada.

My father sharecropped with his dad, while also starting a successful business selling mobile homes. But it was a difficult time for our family. My parents' marriage was under a huge strain. They fought a lot. At one point, my mom threatened to leave my dad. I remember sitting on the couch with my younger brother in our 12' x 60' mobile home on my grandfather's farm. Our parents were in a heated argument. My mom was so angry that she stormed out of the trailer to call her sister to come and pick the three of us up. It was a scene like you might see in a movie. She had my brother in one arm and me in the other, dragging us across the yard to use the phone, which happened to be in her in-laws' house. They were not fans of my mom, which added to the stress of living next to them!

While she was talking on the phone to her sister, I was crying and begging her not to leave my dad. I was so scared of what might happen to our family. I don't know if it was my crying or if my mom was bluffing to get my dad's attention, but she hung up the phone, and we went back to our house on wheels. Just as my brother and I had witnessed them fighting, we now saw them make up. It was a good feeling. But it would not last. In the years to come, their marriage would go through some very turbulent times.

The only good that seemed to come from the move to Canada was a break from the sexual abuse I had been experiencing. However, all the stress of my secrets and my parents' unhappiness were manifesting themselves in the strangest ways. As I mentioned, I was beginning to have a problem with nervous tics.

On one particular occasion, our family was driving back to Canada from visiting our relatives in Michigan. I was really struggling to control my fits. My dad could see me in the rearview mirror of our green Buick station wagon, which someone had given to us. He could hear all the grunts and noises that accompanied my jerky movements. He quickly turned around in anger and ordered me to stop.

"What's the matter with you?!" he shouted. "Are you retarded?"

His angry question hurt. I loved my dad very much. But in that moment, I felt utterly alone and like a complete failure. *Not even my dad loves me*, I thought. I heaped more blame on myself, believing I was the cause of my family's stress and troubles. Why couldn't I control myself?

Because our earthly fathers often project for us the image we have of our heavenly Father, I was sure that God must be upset and disappointed with me as well.

Was He?

One night not long after, while lying on the top bunk in the bedroom I shared with my little brother, I had a dream that was so real I have never forgotten it. It was high definition! It didn't seem like other dreams I had as a kid. It came and left suddenly, and I did nothing but watch and listen. I can still vividly see it in my mind's eye. Everything turned midnight black, and I heard a rushing wind. I could see the wind much like one sees it when an artist brushes glistening streaks on a canvas. Suddenly, the wind stopped. I heard a voice that said, "I am with you." That was it!

The next morning, the dream was all I could think about. Had God visited me in the night? Was He reassuring me that He knew me and that He was with me? I believe so.

How about you? Have you had any God moments? Has God spoken to you in a dream, during a walk, or through another person? Have you ever been reading the Scriptures and had a verse jump off the page and grab your soul? In that instant, did you sense that God was saying something to you?

I believe God has some powerful and transforming things to say to you in this and the following chapters. If you've ever felt or been made to feel like a failure—if you think you're a big disappointment to God—I want you to hear God tell you some very important and significant things about how He feels about you.

I love how Jesus is introduced in Matthew's account of the life and times of the Lord:

> "In the land of Zebulun and of Naphtali, beside the sea, beyond the Jordan River, in Galilee where so many Gentiles live, the people who sat in darkness have seen a great light. And for those who lived in the land where death casts its shadow, a light has shined."
> —Matthew 4:15–16

Imagine what it was like for the common person in Galilee when Jesus came on the scene. Rome dominated and controlled their lives. They were living like slaves in their own land! All the people could do was focus on their oppression. But when Jesus entered their environment, He shifted the focus from the outward to the inward. He revealed how one could be emancipated spiritually, mentally, and emotionally, despite their outward situation. He brought a revolution of the mind and heart that altered how people viewed God, themselves, others, and their environment.

What has enslaved your mind with fear and negativity? Who or what has been controlling your thoughts and ideas? Jesus wants to emancipate you from whatever soul-dominating darkness you're facing. It doesn't matter whether the dark cloud that lingers over you is from your past or if it is a present reality or future threat.

Take a moment to meditate on these God-inspired words:

> "The Word gave life to everything that was created, and his life brought light to everyone. The light shines in the darkness, and the darkness can never extinguish it."
> —John 1:4–5

Think back to Genesis for a moment. How did God give life to everything He created? He spoke life into His creation. How was the world described before God's creative action? Genesis 1:1 says the Earth was formless and void, and darkness was over the face of the deep. Then what?

> "And God said, 'Let there be light,' and there was light. God saw
> that the light was good…"
> —Genesis 1:3–4, NIV

Jesus is the voice and light of God, who wants to speak hope and bring the light of His presence into your whole life. In the context of four components of my Reset strategy, let's see how Jesus brought His transforming presence and power into the lives of His first followers.

Reset 1: Acknowledge That God Chose You

In the first chapter of the Gospel of Mark are some of Jesus's first recorded words:

> "'The time promised by God has come at last!' he announced.
> 'The Kingdom of God is near! Repent of your sins and believe the
> Good News!' One day as Jesus was walking along the shore of
> the Sea of Galilee, he saw Simon and his brother Andrew throw-
> ing a net into the water, for they fished for a living. Jesus called
> out to them, 'Come, follow me, and I will show you how to fish for
> people!' And they left their nets at once and followed him."
> —Mark 1:15

Jesus's call to these ordinary fisherman to leave everything behind and come follow Him reveals a very important principle for your life. I'd like to introduce that principle, and the others I'll be sharing with you in this chapter, in the form of a daily practice as a way of *resetting* how you think of yourself and then others.

Please copy the following phrase in your journal, or use the space provided at the end of this chapter.

Reset #1: Acknowledge that you were chosen by God!

Jesus always chose His followers!

In one of his sermons, renowned pastor Tim Keller emphasizes the fact that Jesus doesn't take volunteers. The reason is that volunteers often show up with an agenda. In the gospel, you will often read about people who were interested in following a Jesus who would allow them to follow Him on their own terms. Keller says that kind of Jesus will never transform anyone's life. Why? Because he's too much like us!

I don't know about you, but I'd rather be *chosen* than be a *volunteer* anyway. To be chosen means someone actually wants you! The apostle Paul talks about the power of being chosen in one of his letters to some Christ followers in Ephesus:

> "Even before he made the world, God loved us and chose us in Christ to be holy and without fault in his eyes. God decided in advance to adopt us into his own family by bringing us to himself through Jesus Christ. This is what he wanted to do, and it gave him great pleasure."
> —Ephesians 1:4–5

Stop and think about this for a couple of minutes: it gave God great pleasure to choose you!

Don't get this wrong! It doesn't mean He found great pleasure in choosing you after you changed or cleaned up your life. It means that God chose you before you did anything! His choosing you has nothing to do with how good or bad you are, how smart or attractive you might be, or how talented and successful you have become.

Growing up, I hated gym class. Maybe you're old enough to remember when the boys had to wear those red athletic short shorts and a white T-shirt. It was the uniform of the day for gym class. As a boy, I was uncoordinated, rather husky (my mom's alternative for the word "fat"—it does sound better, doesn't it?), and lacked confidence. Invariably, during certain units like basketball, we'd end up picking teams. The teacher would stand us up against the gym wall. Two captains would be chosen. They were usually the class jocks, and they would each take a turn picking someone from the lineup to be on their team. One after another, players would be chosen until only a few of us would be left standing against the wall. I lost count of how many times I was the last boy standing. Maybe you've had the same humiliating experience. It was like a huge spotlight was being aimed right at you, wasn't it?

To add insult to injury, sometimes the captain who had no choice but to take me would offer me to the other team. "We don't need Hummel; you can have him!"

"No, we don't need him either!"

Thank God He doesn't treat us that way. In the Creator's mind, every person is a first-round draft pick! There's no comparison or competition. God chooses you because He loves you! His love is unconditional! Do you remember what you already read? Paul said, "It gave him great pleasure" to choose you.

Hebrews 12:2 states, "For the joy set before him he endured the cross, scorning its shame, and sat down at the right hand of the throne of God."

Even though it cost Jesus His life to choose you, it was a joy!

Maybe you're struggling right now to believe all this is true. You may be asking, "How can I personally know that I've been chosen by God?"

I know this is going to sound like an oversimplification, but here's my answer: because it just makes sense!

Before you roll your eyes again, let me explain why I said that. I've shared with you some of the painful parts of my life journey. The difficulties in my life have led to many instances when I've seriously doubted that God has chosen me. In fact, there have been times when I've wondered if God was so disgusted with my life that at some point, He just gave up on me and cast me aside: *Maybe I'm not one of the chosen.* Has that dark thought ever wandered into your consciousness?

In those moments, I step back and ask, *Who am I listening to right now?* In other words, *Who or what is fueling my doubt, fear, or guilt?*

What is the truth?

That question always leads me back to the sacred Scriptures. What does God have to say about me? I have found that God's Word accurately defines and describes the human condition: we are *all* sinners! No one needs to convince me of that. If the word *sin* means to miss the mark of perfection, then I'm a sinner! God explains in His Word why we are all born sinners. I'll cover that in detail in chapter 5, when we talk about identity.

God says none of us can change our sinful human condition on our own. It takes an act of God! In fact, our sin leads to death and eternal separation from God. Rather than leave us in our hopeless condition,

God has come looking for us, to reconcile us back into a relationship with Him.

That's where Jesus comes into the picture. As the Son of God, He took on human flesh and became just like one of us, except without sin. He lived His short human life as the perfect model of what it means to be truly human. How was Jesus treated for all this? He was crucified: So if you've ever felt like you've been mistreated or taken advantage of for doing what is right and loving others, you're not alone!

But when Jesus died, it was more than a good man dying for a good cause. Like a divine sponge, He absorbed the sin, guilt, shame, and condemnation of every human being. Read John 3:16–17: "For this is how God loved the world: He gave his one and only Son, so that everyone who believes in him will not perish but have eternal life. God sent his Son into the world not to judge the world, but to save the world through him."

This means that, according to the Scriptures, your imperfections were transferred to Jesus, and He paid the penalty of death for each one of us. Prior to His death, Jesus promised His followers that He would rise from the dead in three days. His resurrection served as proof of what He accomplished on the cross.

If all this is true, it makes sense that God loves you unconditionally and has chosen you! But if you're still skeptical and wondering, here is my offer to you. I want you to simply live like what I've described is the truth. As you continue reading this book and putting into practice the principles and assignments I give you, see if you experience a transformation in how you think and feel.

God is patient. You don't have to decide right now. Give Him a chance to work in your life.

Reset 2: Focus on God's Purpose for Your Life

Now, if God has chosen you—and I believe that is the case—*what* has He chosen you for? How does He want to transform your life?

In your journal, copy these words next:

> *Reset #2: Dear God, with your help, I aim to reset my focus on Your purpose for my life!*

You may be wondering, What is God's purpose for my life?

Let's read again the words of Jesus in Mark 1:17: "Jesus called out to them, 'Come, follow me…'"

What did that mean for His original listeners? Here's an example from the Bible.

In the tenth chapter of Mark's Gospel, he relates an encounter Jesus had with a young religious leader who was wealthy. The man wanted to know what was required to be assured of eternal life. Jesus told him he must keep the commandments, and the leader responded that he had kept the commandments since boyhood. According to the text, Jesus looked at the guy and genuinely loved him. "There is only one thing you haven't done," Jesus said. He told the leader to go and sell his wealth, give it to the poor, and come follow Him.

The young man's face fell, and "He went away sad because he had many possessions." (See Mark 10:17–22 for the context of the story.)

To follow Jesus means to move forward in obedience and leave behind whatever might interfere with respecting Jesus as one's true leader. The same is true for us today. I believe that Jesus has chosen you and me for the purpose of following Him. Our purpose is simply to follow Jesus, which means living the way He lived.

How did Jesus live? He lived knowing that He was perfectly loved by His Father, just like you are loved by God. When we are secure in God's unconditional love, we are freed to love others in the same way. That kind of love not only changes lives; it changes the world.

How does this all come about? Gradually. The journey with Jesus is a lifelong experience of transformation. It comes about as He retrains our thoughts and ideas, influences our words, and calls us to new behavior.

Reset 3: Surrender to the Spirit Within You

How does He accomplish all that? I'm glad you asked! Look at Mark's Gospel again:

> "John announced: 'Someone is coming soon who is greater than I am—so much greater that I'm not even worthy to stoop down like a slave and untie the straps of his sandals. I baptize you with water, but he will baptize you with the Holy Spirit!' One day Jesus came from Nazareth in Galilee, and John baptized him in the Jordan River. As Jesus came up out of the water, he saw the heavens splitting apart and the Holy Spirit descending on him like

a dove. And a voice from heaven said, 'You are my dearly loved
Son, and you bring me great joy.' The Spirit then compelled Jesus
to go into the wilderness, where he was tempted by Satan for
forty days. He was out among the wild animals, and angels took
care of him."
—Mark 1:7–13

What I want you to notice is that Jesus lived His life in dependence on the presence and power of the Holy Spirit. Jesus was conceived by the power of the Holy Spirit. He was baptized and anointed for ministry by the Holy Spirit. He was led by the Holy Spirit into the wilderness to face and conquer temptation. He continued to be directed by the Holy Spirit throughout His ministry.

According to Hebrews 9:14, it was by the power of the "eternal Spirit" that He was crucified, and Romans 8 conveys that Jesus was raised to life by the Holy Spirit. During His whole life on Earth, God the Son was dependent on God the Spirit.

If you thought the church created the practice of baptism, you may have been surprised to see that John was baptizing people well before Jesus came on the scene. In ancient times, baptism was a rite of passage used by many religions. It carried with it the idea of the past being removed and a new life beginning. For instance, one might be baptized as part of a ritual of leaving one religion for another.

I once baptized my friend, Ken, in the ancient ruins of a city once called Philippi. It is where the apostle Paul baptized a female convert named Lydia. The place where I baptized my friend was near the river where Lydia was baptized. They had created a channel off the river that formed a rushing creek that made its way through a concrete form of a cross. It was quite beautiful. As Ken laid down in the concrete cross, I placed him under the rushing water and baptized him. The rushing water symbolized everything from the past being washed away eternally, leaving behind freshness and newness.

When we put our faith in Christ, the old has passed away, and everything becomes new through the entrance and power of the Holy Spirit.

Just as Jesus lived in the power and presence of the Holy Spirit, you can, too!

Read these verses:

"And now you Gentiles have also heard the truth, the Good News that God saves you. And when you believed in Christ, he identified you as his own by giving you the Holy Spirit, whom he promised long ago. The Spirit is God's guarantee that he will give us the inheritance he promised and that he has purchased us to be his own people. He did this so we would praise and glorify him."
—Ephesians 1:13–14

"And the Holy Spirit helps us in our weakness. For example, we don't know what God wants us to pray for. But the Holy Spirit prays for us with groanings that cannot be expressed in words."
—Romans 8:26

"Don't be drunk with wine, because that will ruin your life. Instead, be filled with the Holy Spirit."
—Ephesians 5:18

"But the Holy Spirit produces this kind of fruit in our lives: love, joy, peace, patience, kindness, goodness, faithfulness, gentleness, and self-control. There is no law against these things."
—Galatians 5:22–23

What do you hear God saying? I hear Him telling you and me that it is impossible to live like Jesus by simply trying to imitate His life. We actually need His Spirit living in us!

I watched a *Superman* movie recently. In it, mild-mannered Clark Kent transforms out of his ordinary business attire into his Superman suit with that unmistakable, great big "S" on his chest! In the 2013 film *Man of Steel*, Superman reveals to Lois Lane that the "S" is not the letter "S" but rather the Kryptonian symbol for hope.

There's a big "S" in your life—the Spirit of God—and He is there to bring you great hope!

But here's the challenge: Many of us never transform out of our ordinary selves. We don't access the supernatural presence of the Spirit of God who lives in us.

When I was a kid, my brother and I liked to get into my dad's car and pretend we could drive. We would take imaginary journeys to all kinds of places while making all the sounds of the engine, brakes, horns, and other instruments. I'm sure it was a silly sight to anyone watching.

That's how I think a lot of us treat our spiritual potential. Even for those of us in the church, we call ourselves Christ followers, we sing about God's presence in our lives, we read the Scriptures, and we listen to the sermons that tell us that we are indwelt by the presence of God, but when it comes to living our lives, we rely on our own power instead. All the power and potential remains untapped in our lives.

Reset Exercise: Surrender to the Spirit, Part 1

I'd like to invite you to try an exercise. If you're not sitting down right now, find a place where you can rest your weight. Take a few deep, cleansing breaths and center yourself.

Begin by focusing on the fact that you are resting all your weight on whatever object you're sitting on. That chair, couch, or stool is bearing you up. I doubt very much you're worried about whether it can bear your weight. You have simply transferred your trust to it.

Now, close your eyes and become aware that you're resting the weight of your life on whatever object you are sitting on. When you're focused, then resume reading.

This exercise is probably pretty easy. In fact, you may have nodded off a bit.

This next exercise is a little more challenging. You're going to use your imagination and let the Holy Spirit *become* whatever you are resting on.

Reset Exercise: Surrender to the Spirit, Part 2

Close your eyes again, and try to see yourself fully transferring the weight of your life to the Holy Spirit. It may be helpful to do some deep breathing, just like a trainer or class leader encourages you to do when you're exercising. With each exhale, surrender more and more to the Spirit until you feel like everything your soul has been carrying is now on Him.

Set the book down, and try the exercise again. Take your time. It might be awkward at first, much like learning to stand on a Bosu ball in the gym. But with practice, it will become natural.

I encourage you to practice this exercise daily so that when you sense you're carrying the weight of the world, you can do it in an instant to reset your focus on the truth.

Let's transfer what you just learned into a daily prayer to focus on. You can write it down in your journal if you like:

Reset #3: Dear God, with your help, I aim to reset my focus daily on becoming more like Jesus by surrendering to your Spirit, who indwells my being.

Let's stop for a moment and summarize in a statement what I believe is becoming true about you: God has chosen you unconditionally for the purpose of being transformed into the image of His Son through the continual presence and power of the Holy Spirit whom you are learning to rest in.

You may want to transfer that to your journal as a personal "I" statement.

Reset Exercise: Visualize Living in the Image of God

Read the statement you wrote in your journal:

God has chosen me unconditionally for the purpose of being transformed into the image of His Son through the continual presence and power of the Holy Spirit whom I am learning to rest in.

Remembering the power of images, can you visualize a picture of what this looks like for you? Try your hand at a bit or art. In your journal, underneath what you wrote, sketch out a scene or a symbol that represents what you just put in print.

If you feel secure enough to share what you drew with someone who will receive you with love and acceptance, tell them what it means to you.

As you practice these and other exercises I give you, you are actually changing your mind/brain connection. Just as physical exercise develops and strengthens muscles, I believe that these trainings are developing new thought patterns, which will birth new ideas and images about God, yourself, and your environment. These exercises activate neuroplasticity. As you develop the right mind muscles, you will stop building the wrong ones! You want the wrong patterns of thinking to atrophy!

Reset 4: Understand That God Is Very Fond of You

You may be struggling deeply right now. You may be finding it hard to believe that God really loves you. For many different reasons, some of us may have developed a mindset that God could not love someone like us. If that is the premise you're beginning with, I understand that it can be hard to find any motivation to change.

So let's focus for a few minutes on changing our minds about God's love.

Let's look at what Mark records again:

> "One day Jesus came from Nazareth in Galilee, and John baptized him in the Jordan River. As Jesus came up out of the water, he saw the heavens splitting apart and the Holy Spirit descending on him like a dove. And a voice from heaven said, 'You are my dearly loved Son, and you bring me great joy.'"
> —Mark 1:9–11

There's a mystery in the Godhead that I cannot explain. How is it that God is one, yet three: Father, Son, and Holy Spirit? No one can adequately explain it. But it is true, and it is an eternal mystery we may never understand. Within the relationship of the One God who is three persons, pure and immeasurable love, pleasure, and joy are continuously being poured out toward each other.

Paul writes in Philippians chapter 2 that when Jesus took on human flesh, He was required to leave the glorified and loving atmosphere He had eternally shared in the Godhead:

> "Though he was God, he did not think of equality with God as something to cling to. Instead, he gave up his divine privileges; he took the humble position of a slave and was born as a human being."
> —Philippians 2:6–7

Though Jesus gave up much to become human like us, there was one thing He brought with Him—the confidence of knowing that His Father loved Him:

> "So Jesus explained, 'I tell you the truth, the Son can do nothing by himself. He does only what he sees the Father doing. Whatever the Father does, the Son also does. For the Father loves the Son and shows him everything he is doing.'"
> —John 5:19–20

Jesus knew His Father loved Him, and He lived in that confidence and motivation.

The eminent theologian N. T. Wright translates the commonly rendered phrase "You are my beloved Son" in John 1:11 to read more accurately, "You are my wonderful son, and you make me very glad."

Do you believe that about yourself? Do you believe it about your friends, spouse, or children? I think many of us struggle to believe it—at least I do. Many times, after behaving badly, I look into the mirror and find it hard to believe that at that moment, God is saying to me, "You're my wonderful child, and you make me very glad!"

Forget about me—I also have a hard time believing that about the people who behave badly in my life! I'm more apt to believe, "You're a real jerk, and you make me mad!"

But God never thinks that way about you or others! What makes God very glad about you has nothing to do with how you perform.

That's the way the world works: you have to do something to be loved, and when you fail to do it or don't do it well enough, you're "unfriended!" God doesn't have any social media accounts, and you never have to worry He's going to unfriend you!

Jesus's substitution for you on the cross makes it possible for God to shower on you the love He has always had for you! You can reject it, but your rejection won't ever stop it. One of the most powerful verses in the gospel of John describes Jesus's attitude on the night He was about to be betrayed:

> "Before the Passover celebration, Jesus knew that his hour had come to leave this world and return to his Father. He had loved his disciples during his ministry on earth, and now he loved them to the very end."
> —John 13:1

"He loved them to the very end." Have you ever thought about what that means? Jesus loved Peter to the very end, even though He knew Peter would deny ever knowing Him—not just once, but three times! And He loved Judas, who betrayed Him! He loved all His disciples, even though He knew they would all run when He needed them the most. He will also love you to the very end!

That's pretty amazing, even if you already knew it!

So our thinking, emotions, and behavior need to be motivated by realizing that God loves us unconditionally and immeasurably—because that's the truth. That's a much better way to be inspired for living, isn't it? What's the alternative? Guilt? Fear? Competition? Be honest with yourself: Isn't that how you are most often motivated to change or improve? Isn't this how parents sometimes try to influence their children? Make them feel bad enough, and they'll stop or change!

Growing up, my whole life was motivated by fear, guilt, and competition. It's probably what exacerbated my OCD.

I feared that if I didn't please God with every thought and choice, He was going to be angry with me. But the harder I tried to please God, the more I could see that I was failing Him.

I don't know how many times I privately shamed myself for my thoughts and actions, thinking that if I hated myself enough, the guilt would push me to do better. The only thing it did was push me down.

When I began playing sports, I found that I could earn compliments and high fives if I performed better than other players. But that's really hard to do when you're picked last and no one ever passes you the ball.

The person who has helped me overcome this wrong thinking and embrace being loved by God more than anyone I know was a former Catholic priest named Brennan Manning. I providentially came to know Brennan through an exchange of letters (yes, letters—not emails). I invited him to come and speak at our church in California, and he did! He spoke for three days, and by the third evening, we literally had people sitting on the floor because there was no room left in the pews. Brennan's message of God's radical love had a deep effect, not only on the congregation I was serving, but also on my heart.

Over the next few years, I stayed in contact with Brennan, and when he came to town, he was gracious enough to invite me for a meal and reflection.

In his book *Abba's Child: The Cry of the Heart for Intimate Belonging*, which I highly recommend you read or reread on this journey, Brennan shares this story:[1]

> Several years ago, Edward Farrell, a priest from Detroit, went on a two-week summer vacation to Ireland to visit relatives. His one living uncle was about to celebrate his eightieth birthday. On the great day, Ed and his uncle got up early. It was before dawn. They took a walk along the shores of Lake Killarney and stopped to watch the sunrise. They stood side by side for a full twenty minutes and then resumed walking. Ed glanced at his uncle and saw that his face had broken into a broad smile. Ed said, "Uncle Seamus, you look very happy."
>
> "I am."
>
> Ed asked, "Why?"
>
> And his uncle replied, "The Father of Jesus is very fond of me."

Try to imagine Uncle Seamus saying it with an Irish accent: "The Father of Jesus is very fond of me." I love those words, don't you? I'm telling you, that's how the Father feels about you, no matter what! The

---

1. Brennan Manning, *Abba's Child: The Cry of the Heart for Intimate Belonging* (Colorado Springs: NavPress, Inc., 2005), 46.

Father of Jesus is so very fond of you because of what His Son did for you!

Manning says if we believe that, it will change our lives:

- It will relax us.
- It will bring us peace.
- It will bring us joy.
- It will change our whole perspective in our relationships with others.

Please write this in your journal:

> *Reset # 4: Dear God, with Your help, I aim to refocus and remind myself daily that You're very fond of me and that I make You glad because of Jesus.*

Reset 5: Focus on Seeing Heaven on Earth

I have one more reality that I want you to begin focusing on. Heaven! Look again at John 1:9:

> "One day Jesus came from Nazareth in Galilee, and John baptized him in the Jordan River. As Jesus came up out of the water, he saw the heavens splitting apart and the Holy Spirit descending on him like a dove."
> —John 1:9

Heaven split apart! The curtain was pulled back. This happened several times in Jesus's life on Earth; for example, see also His Transfiguration (Luke 9). N. T. Wright comments on this concept:

> "Heaven" in the Bible often means God's dimension behind ordinary reality. It's more as though an invisible curtain, right in front of us, was suddenly pulled back, so that instead of the trees and flowers and buildings, or in Jesus's case the river, the sandy desert, and the crowds, we are standing in the presence of a different reality altogether. A good deal of Christian faith is a matter of learning to live by this different reality even when we can't see it. Sometimes, at decisive and climactic moments, the curtain is

drawn back and we see, or hear, what's really going on; but most of the time we walk by faith, not by sight.[2]

Generally speaking, heaven doesn't pull its curtains back and reveal itself to us. But it doesn't make God any less near. He's always with us. David said in Psalm 23, "Even though I walk through the darkest valley, I will not be afraid, for you are close beside me."

What we need at times are eyes of faith to see beyond the veil. On this journey, I want to challenge you to learn how to look behind the curtain and see in your mind the invisible presence of God that surrounds you every moment of your life. I want you to become so focused on the presence of God living in and around you that you will have moments when heaven breaks through in your life.

I want to end this chapter by telling you about another time when heaven broke into my life. My wife and I were newly married and living in Michigan. I thought I would be pursuing an education and experience in the medical field, but God had different and better plans. Through a series of circumstances, He made it clear to my wife and me that I needed to go back to Bible college and finish my degree in theology. So I quit school and prepared to move back to Minnesota to finish a bachelor's degree in Bible and theology.

We didn't have much in those days. We weren't sure how we were going to afford to pay for school or housing. Neither of us had jobs yet. It was a move of faith, and I had my doubts! Was God really in this? Was He really directing me, or had I made this all up in my mind?

I had been volunteering at a youth group at our local church, and it had grown. We loved the kids, and this experience confirmed for us that we belonged in ministry. On our last night with the youth group, they gave us a small money tree, which was a big deal for us poor students! We plucked something like twenty-four dollars off the branches.

A few days later, our church had a missions week emphasis. We had been living in a mobile home on my dad's property, and he had been very generous in providing it at no cost. On Wednesday night of that week, my younger brother, my dad, and I decided to go to church and hear some missionaries tell their stories about God at work on the field.

---

2. N. T. Wright, *Mark for Everyone* (The New Testament for Everyone) (Louisville, Kentucky: Westminster John Knox Press, 2004), 5–6.

I grabbed the wad of twenty-four one-dollar bills and put it in my pocket because I wanted to take my dad and brother out for ice cream. What was I thinking? We needed every dollar we could scrape up! But the love of family and ice cream got the best of me, I guess. At the end of the evening service, the pastor announced that a special offering would be taken for the missionaries.

Guilt! The thought went through my mind, *Put all that money in the plate!* I began to argue with the voice in my head. Surely this wasn't God speaking to me. I even prayed in the pew to God and asked, *Is this really Your voice?* I explained to Him how I had these plans to treat my father and brother to ice cream. We were leaving in a few days! I normally don't hear voices, but on that evening, I heard a familiar voice tell me to put the money in the plate and then head to the restaurant and order the ice cream. I distinctly heard the voice tell me it would be paid for! But I did not believe it. I thought it was just crazy thinking! I kept the money in my pocket and dismissed the whole thing as my imagination.

We left church, went to our favorite ice cream place, and put in our orders. I can still see the three of us sitting there in the booth, enjoying our ice cream sundaes and banana splits. Soon, it was time to leave, and I asked the waitress for the bill. What she said next just about dropped me off my seat onto the floor: "Your bill has already been taken care of. Someone paid it and the tip."

Do you know what I learned that night?

That the Father of Jesus is very fond of me, even when I fail to trust Him!

Here's the last prayer I'd like you to write down in your journal:

Reset #5: Dear God, with Your daily help, I aim to look beyond my earthly circumstances and see heaven dancing with joy around me as I learn to trust Your son and surrender to Your Spirit. Even when I fail!

Chapter 4
Reset Attitude

Recently, my wife and I joined some friends for dinner at a popular spot. We arrived early and had a great table outside, next to a lake. Within an hour, people were walking around, searching for empty tables. Two young ladies approached us and asked if they could have our place when we left. "Just give us the nod. We'll be over there," one said, pointing to a gathering place outside.

When the time came, we gave them the nod. When they showed up, we suddenly found ourselves in a showdown! Another woman had been hawking our spot and believed she owned it because she had waited closer to it. We quickly removed ourselves as a feud broke out over the rights to our table! It doesn't take much to change one's attitude, does it?

Incidentally, my wife called me soon after. We had driven separately, and she had landed a primo parking spot. She told me that a verbal battle broke out between two more parties who thought they had the right to her parking spot! So much for Minnesota Nice!

In the last chapter, we looked at resetting our *focus*. In this chapter, I want to help you reset your *attitude*. I believe the greatest possession you own is your attitude!

Why?

Because your attitude determines what you think and how you feel about God, yourself, and others. It also influences how you feel about the situations you encounter on a daily basis.

Dr. Viktor Frankl was a psychiatrist and philosopher who was rounded up by the Nazis and placed in several different concentration camps during World War II. Unlike so many Jews, he survived the holocaust. During his time in the tortuous camps, he made some very important observations. Here is one of them:

> We who lived in concentration camps can remember the men who walked through the camps comforting others, giving away their last piece of bread. They had been few in number, but they offer sufficient proof that everything could be taken from a man but one thing, the last of human freedoms—to choose one's attitude in any given set of circumstances.[1]

What kind of attitude will you choose to guide your life, relationships, and choices?

Let's get started with a warm-up exercise.

Reset Exercise: Visualize Your Attitude

Take a few minutes to think about how you're feeling about your life right now. What word(s) come to mind? If you were an artist, how would you visually represent your attitude?

Please open your journal and put your thoughts down in words. Leave some space, and then draw the image you have in your mind about how you're feeling.

For example, you might describe your attitude by simply writing down the word "Happy." A smiley face may be all you need to represent your present state of being. Or you may come up with something more descriptive. Maybe you're feeling very inferior today, so you scribble down "Inferior!" You could draw yourself as a child, standing in the shadow of a tall, menacing giant.

Try your hand at describing and drawing what's going on in your mind and heart right now.

---

1. Viktor Frankl, *Man's Search for Meaning* (Boston: Beacon Press, 2017), 69.

What did you come up with? Do you have a positive point of view? Or are you feeling a bit blue? Maybe downright negative? I'm guessing that if you're like most people, your attitude is a bit like the weather here in Minnesota: unpredictable! Is that the case? Do you find that your attitude varies based on how people are treating you? Do your circumstances tend to control your perspective on life?

For most of my life, I've been a slave to my moods. I've allowed people and circumstances to control my viewpoint. As a minister, that can be debilitating! I've often likened being a pastor to being an NFL coach. You're caught between the players (staff and volunteers), the fans (those who sit in the pews and armchair your performance), and the management (the board or council to whom you're accountable). And then there's the owner, God! Add to the mix your spouse, family, neighbors, and strangers, and no wonder it's easy to get a grumpy attitude! No one is exempt.

You cannot directly control the attitude of others, but you can manage your own attitude and indirectly affect the mindset of those around you! As your trainer, I want to help you work on one particular attitude. I believe that when you learn to master this way of thinking, it will significantly change your outlook on life.

Reset 6: Become Willing to Receive Forgiveness

To discover the posture I hope you will adopt, open your training manual (your Bible or Bible app) to the Gospel of Mark. In chapter 2, we encounter four men who bring their paralyzed friend to Jesus to be healed.

"When Jesus returned to Capernaum several days later, the news spread quickly that he was back home. Soon the house where he was staying was so packed with visitors that there was no more room, even outside the door. While he was preaching God's word to them, four men arrived carrying a paralyzed man on a mat. They couldn't bring him to Jesus because of the crowd, so they dug a hole through the roof above his head. Then they lowered the man on his mat, right down in front of Jesus. Seeing their faith, Jesus said to the paralyzed man, 'My child, your sins are forgiven.' But some of the teachers of religious law who were sitting there thought to themselves, 'What is he saying? This is blasphemy!

Only God can forgive sins!'"
—Mark 2:1–7

Jesus had just returned to Capernaum, a fishing village located on the Sea of Galilee that served as His base of operations in the northern regions of Israel. We don't know much about the house where He was staying. Was it borrowed? Rented? Did He build it? He was a carpenter by trade. Does it really matter? You'll see.

The house Jesus was in quickly became crowded by people who were hanging on to His every word. When He spoke, He didn't sound like the other teachers. No, His words were fresh and understandable, and they seemed to breathe life into the minds and hearts of those who listened with any measure of faith. So all kinds of people crammed their way into His home. In fact, they spilled out onto the stones and dirt that made up the thoroughfare around the small houses of the fishing village.

Use your imagination and put yourself in the scene as an onlooker. The four friends of the paralytic are carrying a homemade stretcher tied together with frayed ropes. The bed is sagging from their patient's weight. Who knows how long they've been traveling or how far they have come? All they know is that this Jesus has proven to have the power of God. He made the blind see, the lame walk, the mute speak, and even the dead come to life again! Healing their paralytic friend shouldn't be any problem.

They are just a few meters away from a miracle that will change their friend's life.

But there's a huge obstacle: the crowd! They cannot get through to Jesus. What are their options? They can go home and try again the next day, but how far away is home? It may not be practical. I suppose they could just sit the crowd out and have a picnic while they wait.

What would you do?

What if the person on the cot were your loved one? Your child? Would you be content to just wait it out? Not these guys! They came up with a plan.

As you imagine this scene, notice all the houses have flat roofs. Do you see the stone steps on the sides that go all the way up to the top? That's where they're headed—to the top of the house! What a precarious situation. Can you see them trying to traverse the narrow staircase with their friend in the frayed stretcher? It's almost comical watching them try to negotiate each step without losing their balance or dumping out their friend. What's even more astounding is that no one seems to be noticing. Everyone is engaged in trying to listen to Jesus.

Finally, they're on top! They start tearing apart the roof of the house Jesus was in. Can you imagine what it was like inside the house? Jesus is teaching when He notices this racket above Him. Specks of dust begin to float down in front of His face. Suddenly, the guys on top punch through the ceiling, and Jesus has an instant skylight! Now, everyone in the house, including Jesus, is looking up. The men are awkwardly trying to lower their paralyzed friend down. After a lot of effort, the man is eye level with Jesus.

I wonder what happened when their eyes fastened on each other. If you were the person on the mat looking at Jesus, what expression would you see on His face? Remember, you just ruined the roof of a home and interrupted His teaching. Does Jesus laugh? Look disgusted? Is He elated that you and your friends have expressed such courageous faith? Or does He shake His head in disapproval?

What happens next fills in what the text doesn't necessarily tell us.

Seeing their faith, Jesus said to the paralyzed man, "My child, your sins are forgiven."

What does Jesus mean when He says, "Your sins are forgiven"? I don't think He means forgiven in the sense of, "Ah, don't worry about it. I'm a carpenter; I can fix the roof." No—when He says, "Your sins are forgiven," He's going deep into the man's life. Jesus is addressing the greater need the man has—the need for forgiveness.

"Forgiven?!" I imagine the four friends exclaiming. "We didn't come here for forgiveness. If we wanted forgiveness, we would have gone to the temple in Jerusalem and made the appropriate sacrifices."

If I'm a bystander watching this interchange without any other knowledge about Jesus, I might be thinking *Why is He forgiving the man? Forgiveness isn't going to make him walk again! Besides, isn't that the job of priests?*

"Forgiveness?!" the religious critics were likely exclaiming. "How can He forgive? Only God can forgive! Who does He think He is—God?"

Some of the teachers of religious law who were sitting there thought the same thing: *What is He saying? This is blasphemy! Only God can forgive sins!*

There's one thing I can say for sure: I would have felt disappointed if I had lugged my friend up to, and through, a roof to be healed and simply heard he was forgiven. Have you ever been disappointed by God? Have you ever come to God with a prayer request, only to feel like He either can't hear you or doesn't care?

This may be a good time to write down some of your disappointments with God. I've had my share! I've mentioned to you my mother's death. I was so disappointed that God allowed her to suffer such pain and fear before she died. After all her years of missionary service and enduring many challenges, why didn't God take her in a more dignified way?

Reset Exercise: Face Disappointment

Have you ever been disappointed by God? Have you ever come to God with a prayer request only to feel like He either can't hear you or doesn't care?

Be honest, and describe your disappointments in your journal.

By the way, if you're feeling guilty about feeling disappointed, remember that some of God's best servants felt let down by God. Read Luke 7:18–35 sometime. Jesus's own cousin, known as John the Baptist, was sitting in a dungeon and sent word through his disciples to Jesus to ask, "Are you really the Son of God, or should we be looking for someone else?"

Previously John had boldly declared that Jesus was the "Lamb of God who takes away the sin of the world!" (John 1:29). But in prison, John was smothered by the shadows of doubt! If Jesus was the Messiah capable of doing all kinds of miracles, why didn't He use His power to free John? Everyone else was experiencing freedom. *Hey, I'm Your cousin, the guy who introduced you!*

Jesus's response to John, in Luke 7, amounts to, "Tell John I am bringing freedom to a lot of people, and add this: God blesses those who do not fall away (or in Greek, "trip") because of me." In other words, tell John not to trip over the fact that I may not rescue him from prison.

It's one thing to acknowledge our disappointments with God, but we have to be careful they don't become a stumbling block to our spiritual development and maturity as Christ's followers. I could complain to God about a lot in my past. Why did He let me be abused? Why didn't He change circumstances in my family? Why OCD? It's one thing to lament our sorrows and letdowns, but we can't get stuck there. Something greater is taking place.

Let's rejoin the story.

Just like the friends had punched a hole through Jesus's roof, Jesus was punching holes, too—in people's views and beliefs. For instance, thank God He didn't just heal this man's paralysis and then tell him to go home. What if Jesus had just looked at him and said, "Oh man, this is impressive. Love the faith. You're healed—get up and go home." Everyone (well, nearly everyone, except the grumpy theologians) would have been amazed and ready to vote Jesus in as king! The guy and his friends would have been jumping, dancing, singing, and rejoicing! "I'm healed, I'm healed, hooray and hallelujah! Yeshua is the real deal!"

But in reality, it would be a very sad outcome! Why? Even though the man would be physically healed, he would still be spiritually sick! It would be a cruel trick. "I've made you physically well, but spiritually, you're still far from God."

It was out of sincere love that Jesus made it His priority that day to heal the man of a worse type of paralysis: the paralysis of the soul. The paralyzed man's biggest problem is our biggest problem. It is never our suffering, but our sin. That is what Jesus came to do: take care of the sin problem. We may not always get our physical needs met, but we can always get our sin needs met.

Also, Jesus's miracles were never meant to be an end in themselves. They were meant to prove who He was:

"'But I have a greater witness than John—my teachings and my miracles. The Father gave me these works to accomplish, and they prove that he sent me.'"
—John 5:36

And in the story about the paralyzed man, listen to what Jesus says:

"Jesus knew immediately what they were thinking, so he asked

them, 'Why do you question this in your hearts? Is it easier to say
to the paralyzed man "Your sins are forgiven," or "Stand up, pick
up your mat, and walk"? So I will prove to you that the Son of Man
has the authority on earth to forgive sins.' Then Jesus turned to
the paralyzed man and said, 'Stand up, pick up your mat, and go
home!' And the man jumped up, grabbed his mat, and walked out
through the stunned onlookers. They were all amazed and praised
God, exclaiming, 'We've never seen anything like this before!'"
—Mark 2:8–12

Being forgiven is much more important than being physically
healed. It is more significant than money, success, sex, or anything else
that our culture values as the end-all. As a victim of abuse, I can tell
you that being forgiven is even more important than anything that has
been done to you! Despite the injustices you may have faced in life, for
which you are *not* to blame, you still need forgiveness.

Why? Because as we learned in the last chapter, we are all sinners.
We all fall short of perfection, which is the only way we can be right
with God. Because we cannot make it right with God by any effort
of our own, we are left to His mercy. Because God is a just God who
cannot simply excuse our guilt, He must accept His Son as a substitute
for us. And because Jesus takes our place and our condemnation, we
can be forgiven and treated as though we never sinned. The Bible calls
this *justification*.

Many years ago, I heard a story that gave me insight into this miracle
called justification. It goes something like this:

A man in England put his Rolls-Royce on a boat and went across to
the continent to go on a holiday. While he was driving around Europe,
something happened to the motor of his car. He cabled the Rolls-Royce
people back in England and said, "I'm having trouble with my car;
what do you suggest I do?"

Well, the Rolls-Royce people flew a mechanic over! The mechanic
repaired the car, flew back to England, and left the man to continue
his holiday.

As you can imagine, the fellow was wondering, *How much is this
going to cost me?* So when he got back to England, he wrote the Rolls-
Royce people a letter and asked how much he owed them. He received
a letter from the office that read, "Dear Sir: There is no record anywhere

in our files that anything ever went wrong with a Rolls-Royce."

That's justification! Isn't that fantastic?

Which is easier to say: "You're forgiven" or "You're physically healed"? Tim Keller makes a point in one of his sermons that when Jesus heals someone, He speaks. He speaks, and the leper is cleansed, the lame person walks, the mute speaks, and the dead are raised to life again. But to forgive, says Keller, is infinitely harder; it will require that God's Son must die! It's really costly to forgive.

If Jesus had to die on the cross to forgive us, you may be wondering, how could He forgive the paralyzed man before He died on the cross? Here's the way I look at it. Jesus could forgive on Earth because He knew He would go to the cross to make forgiveness possible. All people had to do was exercise faith in His word and authority. By their faith, they were granted early forgiveness!

Imagine a friend calls you up and says, "I want to buy you a new home. Please go ahead and choose a house you like and put a deposit on it. Let me know how much it is, and I'll send the funds." You go in search of a house, find one, and purchase it by putting down some earnest money. You do this because you have faith in your friend's word that he will make good on his promise. That's how these people received their forgiveness prior to Jesus's death on the cross.

The attitude that makes all the difference is forgiveness. The first step is to begin looking past those disappointments you may have and start focusing on the greater miracle of God's forgiveness.

I invite you to write this statement down in your journal:

Reset #6: Dear God, I thank You for Your attitude of forgiveness toward me. I pray that You will help me establish a daily mindset of being forgiven instead of disappointed.

I believe the willingness to receive forgiveness is the most important attitude you can have in your life. Tim Keller says, "It is as though Jesus is saying, 'I'm the only savior that if you get me will fulfill you and if you fail me will forgive you.'" I love that! Do you? Really think about this for a minute. Will money forgive you? Will sex, success, politics, or talent give you absolution of your past? No way! But Jesus will.

Reset 7: Receive and Celebrate Your Forgiveness

Let's get personal now. I want you to receive your own forgiveness from our Father in heaven. Please write this in your journal:

Reset #7: Dear Father God, regardless of my feelings or what has ever been said or taught to me, I aim to practice receiving and celebrating Your forgiveness in my life.

Earlier in the book, I taught you about neuroplasticity, or the ability to literally change the brain. To do that, you have to begin thinking differently, which means more than just telling yourself, "This is how I must start to think."

Earlier, we also talked about the power of images, created by the imagination. Scientists have proven that if you imagine a spider crawling up your leg, your body will react with the same sensations you'd feel if it were actually happening, even though it's not! So to be able to experience God's forgiveness, I want to suggest a very simple exercise.

Reset Exercise: Wash Away Your "Should"

Whenever you shower, take a few minutes to stand under the water as it pours over you. Bring to mind the specific things that make you feel condemned or guilty. For instance, there is a Pharisee in my mind who regularly likes to accuse and condemn me for things I've said or done in the past. I have to remind myself in those moments of the truth that God has forgiven and forgotten the old sins I've confessed. I let the water wash away the condemning voice and instead focus on my freedom.

As another example, I sometimes struggle with self-hatred. I think, *I should be a better person; I should serve more, give more, be kinder, etc.* As I stand under the shower, I let the water cleanse all the "should" in my life away!

What sins or "should" do you need to let go of?

Once you have them clearly in mind, recite this prayer, or one like it in your own words:

> *Father, as I place myself beneath the cleansing power of this water, I thank You for placing me under the forgiving power of Your love and grace. I receive Your eternal forgiveness.*

You may be wondering, *Don't I have to confess my sins to be forgiven? Doesn't it say something like that in the Bible?*

Yes, it does. I don't know if this is the verse you're thinking of, but it's pretty plain and to the point:

> "But if we confess our sins to him, he is faithful and just to forgive
> us our sins and to cleanse us from all wickedness."
> —1 John 1:9

It makes me think of the old riddle, "Which came first—the chicken or the egg?" I think I know the answer, spiritually speaking! I believe the forgiveness of God precedes repentance.

You may be familiar with the story of the prodigal son. If not, check it out in your Bible, in Luke 15:11–31. In this parable, Jesus describes an ungrateful son who tells his father to give him his inheritance. It's the equivalent of saying, "I wish you were dead." The son then leaves home and spends everything he has on wild living, until there's nothing left. To complicate things further, there's a severe famine in the land, and the only work the son can find is feeding pigs. Given that Jesus's audience were Jews, I assume the young man in Jesus's story is one, too. So you can imagine the indignity of this son's position and how low a point he had reached!

He finally decided to go home and seek his father's mercy. He planned out his speech and intended to simply ask if his father would hire him as one of the servants on the farm. He doesn't believe that he deserves sonship again.

Let's pick up the story in Jesus's own words:

> "So he returned home to his father. And while he was still a long
> way off, his father saw him coming. Filled with love and compas-
> sion, he ran to his son, embraced him, and kissed him. His son said
> to him, 'Father, I have sinned against both heaven and you, and I

am no longer worthy of being called your son.' But his father said to the servants, 'Quick! Bring the finest robe in the house and put it on him. Get a ring for his finger and sandals for his feet. And kill the calf we have been fattening. We must celebrate with a feast, for this son of mine was dead and has now returned to life. He was lost, but now he is found.' So the party began.'"
—Luke 15:20–24

Before the son could get out his confession and plan, he was smothered in the love and forgiveness of his father! It was the compassion of the father that restored the young man to full sonship. In the father's eyes, his offspring had never stopped being his son.

For most of my young life, I was scared of God because He was always represented to me as angry, with His fists on His hips and a stern, disappointed look on His face. I often wondered if I had repented hard enough to receive His forgiveness. I used to think after repeating the same offenses so many times that maybe I had used up God's reservoir of mercy. Why or how could God tolerate the likes of me? My OCD and ruminating tendencies plays into the hands of the spiritual enemy, who loves to throw down blows of accusations. There have been times when I've felt like the sin mess of my past and my foibles in the present are beyond God's patience and mercy. Maybe you feel the same way.

Let me tell you a dirty story! Hold your breath—it really stinks. We were new parents, and my wife was pregnant with our second child. She happened to be away one afternoon while I stayed home to keep an eye on our firstborn. He was supposed to be upstairs, asleep in his crib. However, he woke up from his nap and managed to climb over the rail and onto the white carpeted floor of the townhouse we were renting.

He was stealthy; I didn't hear him upstairs. Those sound machines are not always helpful.

I looked at the clock on the wall and thought he'd been sleeping a long time, so I decided to go check on him. I quietly crept up the stairs and approached the door to his bedroom. I slowly opened it, expecting him to be asleep on his bed, but instead my senses were assaulted with a foul odor and the disturbing sight of seeing him smear his poop across the wall!

"Oh no!" I exclaimed. Poo (not the bear, Pooh, though!) was everywhere! I discovered that he'd been redecorating his room while I thought he was peacefully asleep. I stood in bewilderment. The poo was in the once-white carpet, on the walls, in his hair, and all over his body! It was so gross! I gagged as I picked him up and held him as far away as I could. I carried his stubby little body and dangling legs to the shower. I now had his stuff on the bottom of my feet and on my arms and hands.

Where was my wife when I needed her? It took a really long time to clean him up. Then came the daunting task of cleaning the carpet, walls, and door. Meanwhile, he was back in his playpen, clean, dry, and seemingly entertained as he watched me gag my way through cleansing the room of his mess!

So, what's the point? I loved him before he made the mess, I loved him when he made the mess, I loved him while I cleaned up his mess—and I still love him many messes later!

We've all made and sometimes still make sinful messes. But God stepped in, and through the loving sacrifice of Jesus, has cleansed us from every mess—past, present, and future!

I don't know if it was PTSD from his early childhood experience, but as our son grew older, he started having an aversion to getting dirty. He particularly hated sticky hands! We would be out at a restaurant, and if his hands got the least bit sticky, he'd start crying and begging to be cleaned! What a reversal. The hands that once used poo to make murals now can't stand getting dirty! What happened? He was beginning to understand the difference between clean and dirty, and clean felt much better!

When you encounter the grace and truth of God, you begin to realize how unclean sin is. As the Holy Spirit uses the truth of God to convict you of the sin dirt in your life, you want to take a shower in His loving mercy and grace. When God confronts us with sin, it is out of love. He sees where it will lead us and how it will cripple or ruin our lives. So He holds up the mirror of His truth through His Word. But wait a minute: What does He want us to see in the mirror? Is the purpose of the mirror to reveal how dirty we are? Or is the mirror meant to reveal the image beneath the dirt?

Is it time for a shower?

Reset 8: Practice a Forgiving Attitude Toward Others

So far, we've talked about being loved and forgiven by God. But what about becoming a forgiving person? It's one thing to receive pardon, but are we willing to offer pardon to those who offend us? Are you willing to develop your forgiveness muscle?

How does one do that? Let's continue observing Jesus's words and actions in Mark 2:

> "Then Jesus went out to the lakeshore again and taught the crowds that were coming to him. As he walked along, he saw Levi son of Alphaeus sitting at his tax collector's booth…"
> —Mark 2:13–14a

Capernaum bordered two little kingdoms controlled by two sons of the deceased king, Herod the Great. Anytime someone passed between the two domains, a tax would be collected. Levi was working the toll booth as one of the tax collectors when Jesus called him out!

> "'Follow me and be my disciple,' Jesus said to him. So Levi got up and followed him."
> —Mark 2:14b

> "Later, Levi invited Jesus and his disciples to his home as dinner guests, along with many tax collectors and other disreputable sinners. (There were many people of this kind among Jesus' followers.)"
> —Mark 2:15

The Greek word used to describe the "disreputable sinners" literally means preeminent sinners—those who were known for their vices, such as tax collectors, prostitutes, and thieves. They were viewed as traitors and the worst kind of humans. Read the reaction of the religious elite:

> "But when the teachers of religious law who were Pharisees saw him eating with tax collectors and other sinners, they asked his disciples, 'Why does he eat with such scum?' When Jesus heard this, he told them, 'Healthy people don't need a doctor—sick people do. I have come to call not those who think they are righteous, but those who know they are sinners.'"
> —Mark 2:16–17

Pay attention once again to verse 15. I want to point out something that may not seem very important, but I think it is. In the original language, Levi is never mentioned in that verse. Here is how the English Standard Version accurately renders it:

> "And as he reclined at table in his house, many tax collectors and sinners were reclining with Jesus and his disciples, for there were many who followed him."
> —Mark 2:15, ESV

The assumption of the translators of other versions of the Bible, like the NIV or the NLT (my favorite), assume that Jesus went to Levi's house, so they insert his name. But it's not always wise to assume things. According to the eminent scholar N. T. Wright in his commentary on this passage, this is Jesus's house, not Levi's! I agree.

You may be asking, *What's the point?* Here it is. As one scholar put it, one of the striking features of Jesus's ministry was the meals He shared with sinners, especially social outcasts. Pharisees and religious-minded people avoided the unclean at all costs. No decent person would eat a meal with such scum of the Earth. Why? Because in the East, when you eat a meal, it is more than just sharing food; it is a sign of friendship or the desire for friendship!

I travel often to Israel, and there is a Palestinian man whom I've befriended over the years. He runs a little store near Jericho, and whenever I'm in the area, I make it a point to see him and bring him much-needed business from the tours I lead. He's a giant of a man, with size 17 feet! It is very hard for him to find shoes or sandals that fit. So every time I go, I take him a new pair. I love this guy! Our relationship has now evolved to the point that he wants me to go home with him and have a meal. It is the greatest honor I could ever receive because what he is saying to me is, "I want you to be part of my family!"

This concept is also true in the Orthodox Jewish culture, even today. For instance, if an Orthodox Jew invites you over to his home for a meal, he is inviting you to his *Mikdash Me'at*, or miniature temple. That's a very special privilege; he must think very highly of you!

That's why seeing this house as the house of Jesus instead of the house of Levi is so important. Jesus has invited the worst and most despicable sinners into His little temple! He's saying to them, "I want to be friends with you." It was scandalous!

How do you know when the nature of God's forgiveness has taken over your life? As you become more nonjudgmental of yourself, your judgment of others diminishes.

Can we be honest at this point and admit we all struggle with being critical and disapproving of others? We do it effortlessly, like breathing.

Who have you judged today?

The person who cut you off in traffic? *What a jerk! Who taught him or her to drive?*

The woman wearing that ridiculous outfit? *It clashes; she has no sense of fashion or modesty!*

The guy with tattoos that looked like flames creeping up his neck? *I'll bet he's on drugs or something.*

Maybe it was someone who seemed out of place in your neighborhood. *I wonder if he's casing the homes on our street.*

Or was it the guy or gal at the corner holding up a sign asking for money? *Get a job; McDonald's is hiring!*

Reset Exercise: Face Judgment of Others

Please open your journal again and write down whom you've judged in the past twenty-four hours. Even if you don't know their name(s), you can write something like, "The moron who kept me waiting at the green arrow in traffic!" Be honest, and take your time.

Why do we judge others? Psychologists say we tend to point out faults in others that we don't like in ourselves. Look again at your judgment list. How are the people you've been hard on like you? Another reason we judge others is to feel better about ourselves. I see a lot of this among immature followers of Jesus. Like miniature Pharisees, they walk around gossiping about the shortcoming of others to make themselves feel superior and spiritual. I find this attitude in myself, too. Sometimes, I'll hear a gifted speaker and feel threatened and then proceed to criticize that person's style in my mind. God, forgive me!

Does this prohibition against judging mean we're never supposed to point out the wrongs of others? No, it doesn't mean that. You have to speak the truth when it's appropriate. It is not loving to let someone misbehave if you can help them see their wrong and make it right. But here's the important question: What's your motive? What is the intention behind confronting another person about his or her faults? If our motive is to make another person feel guilty or ashamed, then we have no business saying anything.

Our job is not to act as their judge. Nor is it our responsibility to condemn! Our responsibility is to point others to the truth in the most humble and loving way possible. If I'm going to point out your wrong, I need to keep in mind all my own faults. My aim is to approach confronting someone else with the motive of reconciliation and forgiveness that abounds from the joy of having experienced being forgiven.

Brennan Manning writes, "At the foot of the cross we recognize ourselves as forgiven enemies of God and are empowered to extend forgiveness and reconciliation…As long as we continue to live as if we are what we do, as if we are what we have, and as if we are what other people think about us, we will remain filled with judgments, opinions, evaluations, and condemnations…"[2]

He continues, quoting Henri Nouwen: "Only when we claim the love of the crucified Christ with heartfelt conviction, the love that transcends all judgments, can we overcome all fear of judgment. When we have become completely free from the need to judge others, we will also become completely free from the fear of being judged.…The experience of not having to judge cannot coexist with the fear of being judged, and the experience of the nonjudgmental love of the crucified Savior cannot coexist with a need to judge others."[3]

Please write this down in your journal:

Reset #8: Dear God, help me to begin practicing a forgiving attitude toward others rather than a judgmental opinion. Help me to see others in the same light that You see me.

But how do you forgive someone who never says they're sorry? How

---

2. Manning, *Signature of Jesus*, 59.
3. Ibid., 61.

do you pardon someone who has devastated your life? It takes an act of God, literally! Close to the time of Jesus's death, He said to His followers, "So now I am giving you a new commandment: Love each other. Just as I have loved you, you should love each other" (John 13:34).

The key to understanding that verse is to read what took place in the upper room in the prior thirty-three verses. John 13 begins by telling us how much Jesus loved His disciples: "Before the Passover celebration, Jesus knew that his hour had come to leave this world and return to his Father. He had loved his disciples during his ministry on earth, and now he loved them to the very end" (John 13:1).

He loved Peter to the very end, even though He knew Peter would promise to never abandon Him and then deny Him three times. Jesus loved Judas to the very end, even though Judas plotted and sold Jesus out to the enemy. Interestingly, when Judas showed up later to identify Jesus so the guards could arrest Him, Jesus called him a friend. The fact is, all the disciples ran out on Jesus when He needed them the most—but He still loved them to the very end!

One of the most powerful pictures in the upper room is when Jesus washed the feet of each of His disciples. Washing feet was the responsibility of the lowliest servant in the household. But as Luke tells us in his account, the disciples were arguing among each other that night about who was going to be the greatest! So Jesus got up from the table and took on the menial task with a sense of love and humility.

Years ago, my mentor, Haddon Robinson, said, "It's really hard to wash someone's feet when they're kicking you in the teeth!"

That's me! I was there in that upper room on the night when Jesus was betrayed. I, too, have kicked Him in the teeth. You might ask, "How?" When I refuse to forgive, even though He has forgiven me, it's a kick in the teeth. When I knowingly choose to disobey His Word because I want to satisfy my own desires, it's a kick in the teeth. When I don't believe I'm worthy to receive His grace, it's a kick in the teeth. Yet when I do things like this, He still bends down to wash my feet with His love!

Here's the key: until you've had Jesus wash your feet with His love, it is almost impossible to wash the feet of anyone else.

Here's your final exercise for this session.

Reset Exercise: Receive Forgiveness to Give Forgiveness

Find a quiet space where no one will interrupt you. Fill a bowl or basin with water. Sit in a chair, and place your feet in the water. Read John 13:1–34 with your feet in the water. Now close your eyes and imagine Jesus is there, kneeling before you and pouring water over your feet. Each movement of His hand signifies His love and forgiveness of your sins. Receive His love and forgiveness. Be still and worship Him.

When you can receive His full forgiveness and begin to exercise the same kind of forgiveness towards others, this attitude of forgiveness will begin to reset your attitude in all the circumstances of your life.

Chapter 5
Reset Identity

In my freshman year of high school, I decided it was time to toughen up, so I joined the wrestling team. I figured that because my brother and I were always wrestling on the living room floor, I might as well try competing. The only thing I didn't think through was the fact that my brother was four years younger and much lighter than me. I quickly found out that wrestling my peers was a lot harder. In fact, it was humiliating.

I barely survived my first year of wrestling, but something good came of it: I lost weight! That spring, when my mom and aunt took me shopping at JCPenney for my annual Easter suit, I didn't have to try on clothes for "husky boys."

That spring, I decided to join the track team. After making the team, the coach told me I'd be running the mile. I may have lost weight wrestling, but I had not gained speed!

One race in particular will always stay in my mind. On a cool, rainy day at Bulldog Stadium, we were hosting our annual track invitational. That meant there were more fans in the stands than usual. A lot of kids that day had one or both of their parents there to cheer them on. My mom never attended any of my sporting events, and my dad rarely made an appearance. In their minds, sports were dangerous and a waste of time.

My mom worried I'd get injured, and my dad said if I wanted to get in shape, I should quit school and work for him. He was serious!

Actually, now that I think of it, maybe he was using reverse psychology because the thought of spending the rest of my life working for my dad made me want to stay in school!

It was finally time for the mile race, and we all lined up. Because it was an invitational, the track was quite crowded, and I was positioned toward the back of the group. The gun popped, and off we went. The speed of the pack made me run a faster pace than I was used to, and half a mile into the competition, I was spent! As I began the fourth and final lap around the quarter-mile track, the winner crossed the finish line! Do you know what that means? I had nearly been lapped in the mile!

As I came around the last turn and the final 220 yards, my lungs were burning, and my legs felt numb. The only pain worse than that was the fact I was the only competitor left on the track. Everyone else had finished the race! As I looked down the home stretch, I saw the track coach standing there with his arms folded across his chest and a disgusted look on his face.

As I crossed the finish line, I wandered onto the grass field in the middle of the track, barely able to stand. I was exhausted and ashamed. A voice in my head told me I had let the coach, the team, and the people in the stands down. I just wanted to disappear.

Then suddenly, I felt two strong arms enfold me and pull me in tight. *Who was it?* I wondered. I knew it wasn't my dad, and it certainly wasn't the track coach! Who was holding me up when I wanted to fall down? Finally, I felt release and looked up. It was Blake Erickson, my wrestling coach and a science teacher. Coach Erickson was a man of few words, and nothing needed to be spoken that day. His hug said it all.

Reset 9: Acknowledge That God Loves You Unconditionally, No Matter What

If there are defining moments in a person's life, that was one of the first for me. All these years later, I'm still moved when I relive that moment in Bulldog Stadium.

Why? Because I experienced someone unconditionally accepting me, even though I had been branded a loser.

I have always struggled with finding my identity, with truly knowing who I am. It's hard to find yourself when the people around you are constantly trying to define who they think you are. But that's an inescapable part of life. Every one of us is shaped by our environment.

I guess you could say we're a bit like Play-Dough; people are constantly trying to squeeze us into their idea of who they think we should be or become. But what happens when we don't fit the mold, or when our clay is inferior to their design? Think about the people who try to shape our lives, even those with the best intentions.

For instance:

- **Our parents have a huge say in how we see ourselves.** Most of the time, it's good, but sometimes, such as when they're frustrated, their efforts fall short and can even be damaging, like when my father angrily asked me if I was retarded. He must have thought making me feel bad might cure me of my incessant tics, and I'd be more normal.

- **Our peers probably have more influence on how we view ourselves than anyone else, especially during our younger years.** Students want to fit in and belong, and when they're rejected or ridiculed, they are devastated. When kids bullied me in junior high and made fun of my looks and weight, I formed a very negative narrative in my mind about who I was. I came to believe that I was fat, ugly, and stupid.

- **Teachers, coaches, and counselors also shape our self-image.** While I did have some positive models in my life like Coach Erickson, I also had some teachers and coaches who were anything but positive. I remember after doing poorly on some standardized tests, the guidance counselor at our high school "encouraged" me not to go to college and look at alternatives.

- **The media!** What positive messages do the media send us these days? I am so thankful the world of media was limited in many ways when I was in my developing years. My heart goes out to parents and students who must combat the confusing messages that come by way of the internet and social media, not to mention print and television.

- **Church—yes, even the church gets into the act.** What messages do we get from church about who we're supposed to be and how we're to behave? My church experience growing up left me feeling ashamed, guilty. and hopeless. Even though we sang songs about grace, I rarely saw the people exercise it in their attitudes or relationships towards each other. I still wonder at times how I ever became a pastor.

So, who are you? How do you see yourself?

Reset Exercise: How Do You See Yourself?

I have a little exercise I want you to do, but first, carefully read the instructions.

You're going to write down a very simple phrase in your journal and then complete a statement. It is very important that you are raw and honest. Don't write down what you *think* you should write. Instead, finish the statement based on how you really feel about yourself at this moment.

Here you go. Write down and complete this phrase:

Right now, I see myself as _____.

How do you feel about what you wrote?

You may be perfectly content with how you see yourself right now. If so, great! But will you be content with yourself next week? Next year? On the other hand, you may be looking at what you wrote and thinking *Ahh, I feel like such a wreck. I don't like who I am, but who am I supposed to be?*

Keep reading because you're going to find hope!

Reset 10: Know That You Are Created in the Image of God

As I write this chapter, I'm in the country of Jordan, visiting people who have been branded as refugees. The community of faith I have the privilege to lead has generously invested in helping bring relief and hope to some of the most marginalized people on the planet.

I remember the first time I visited the refugees in Jordan, I had the opportunity to hear from some of these displaced people. One man in particular had a profound effect on me. He stood in front of us and said passionately, "When you go home, please tell your people that we are not refugees! We are human beings, just like you!"

What does it mean to be a human being? A person?

If I'm not what my family, culture, government, or the media label me, then who am I? From where do I draw my identity?

You may be reading this and thinking, *I'm just going to be myself!* The truth is, we have less control over "being ourselves" than we may think. Of course, we can make choices about how we think, look, and behave, but the palette of colors available to us has been influenced by others!

Does that mean we don't have a true self-identity? Are we just a product of our environment?

My daughter has taken a heartfelt interest in the ancestry of our family and has done some pretty extensive research to recreate our ancestral tree. Recently, she discovered that one of the branches of our heritage can be traced all the way back to Emperor Charlemagne! Hey, I'm not a mutt after all! I've got royalty flowing through my veins. Maybe I'll move to Europe and reclaim what is rightfully mine!

You are about to find out that you have more than royalty to claim as your identity. Forget about what society says about you! Refuse to live under the labels and metaphors others have hung over your life. Look at what the Creator thinks about you!

"Then God said, 'Let us make human beings in our image, to be like us. They will reign over the fish in the sea, the birds in the sky, the livestock, all the wild animals on the earth, and the small animals that scurry along the ground.' So God created human beings in his own image. In the image of God he created them; male and female he created them. Then God blessed them and said, 'Be fruitful and multiply. Fill the earth and govern it. Reign over the fish in the sea, the birds in the sky, and all the animals that scurry along the ground.'"
—Genesis 1:26–28

Do you want to know who you really are? You are one who has been created in the image of God! You are the Imago Dei!

If you're wondering if this is really true, you're not alone. I've wondered the same thing. Countless times, I've looked in the mirror and thought, *If I'm really created in the image of God, where is that likeness? Why don't I see the Imago Dei in my reflection?*

The answer invites us back to the beginning, where we can discover our original likeness. Unfortunately, we also learn how what we had was lost. The rest of the Bible's story is how God has pursued His creation with the intention of restoration. We can have our first likeness restored!

To ensure you get the most out of this chapter, I'm going to ask you to join me in doing some intentional doodling. I know it may sound a bit strange, but it's actually a warm-up exercise for your brain. If we're going to reset how we think, we need to start prodding our brains to look at things differently.

The doodling we're going to do will help your brain see, discover, and retain some things it might ordinarily miss merely by reading an explanation. This exercise will also help prepare you for the important exercises that come in the second half of this chapter. I really want this chapter to change your self-image!

Are you ready?

Reset Exercise: Find Your Center

Let's begin exploring what it means to be created in God's image. The Lutheran theologian and martyr Dietrich Bonhoeffer tried to answer the question this way: "As the image of God, man draws his life entirely from his origin in God..."[1]

What does that mean? Get your journal and whatever you want to use to sketch with, and write the name of God in large block letters, like this:

GOD

---

1. Bonhoeffer, *The Cost of Discipleship*, 22.

Inside the O, draw your version of Adam and Eve. Anyone who knows me knows that although I'm a wannabe artist, my talent seems to have peaked at stick figures. If you can do better, go for it!

Are you finished?

What is your rendering of Adam and Eve in the O of God supposed to mean? In this exercise, the O stands for "origin." According to lexico.com, *origin* is defined as "the point or place where something begins, arises, or is derived." In other words, human beings were created by God, from God, and for God. In God, one is able to truly know Him. It is also in God that a person can really know themselves, others, and the totality of God's creation.

Next, I want you to add four arrows outward from the O, pointing in four different directions, to symbolize the first couple's knowledge of everything emanating from God as their center.

How's your brain doing? Are you beginning to see things a bit differently?

My friend and theologian, Dr. Christopher Yuan, brings out a really important point in his book *Holy Sexuality and the Gospel*. When the Bible says we are created in the image of God, it includes each person's total self, the whole being. The image of God is not some part of us, but the sum of who we are![2]

Genesis 1:31 tells us that after God created humankind, here is what He did next: "Then God looked over all he had made, and he saw that it was *very good*" (emphasis mine).

But that's exactly what I wonder about when I look in the mirror! Where is that God-given goodness in my life? Why is it so hard to find in the world around me? What happened to all the goodness?

Reset 11: Regain Your Stolen Identity

The answer is evil! Evil showed up in paradise. The serpent, however you want to interpret the meaning of that creature, suggested to our first parents they did not need God to be their origin. They could derive life from themselves. In fact, he told them they could determine what was *really* good and evil. Why should God have the say?

That led to one of the biggest heists in history. Adam and Eve stole their own identity by disobeying the will of God:

> "The LORD God placed the man in the Garden of Eden to tend and watch over it. But the LORD God warned him, 'You may freely eat the fruit of every tree in the garden—except the tree of the knowledge of good and evil. If you eat its fruit, you are sure to die.'"
> —Genesis 2:15–17

Here's how it all went down:

> "The serpent was the shrewdest of all the wild animals the LORD God had made. One day he asked the woman, 'Did God really say you must not eat the fruit from any of the trees in the garden?'
> 'Of course we may eat fruit from the trees in the garden,' the woman replied. 'It's only the fruit from the tree in the middle of the garden that we are not allowed to eat. God said, "You must not

2. Dr. Christopher Yuan, *Holy Sexuality and the Gospel*, 17.

eat it or even touch it; if you do, you will die.'"
'You won't die!' the serpent replied to the woman. 'God knows that
your eyes will be opened as soon as you eat it, and you will be
like God, knowing both good and evil.'
The woman was convinced. She saw that the tree was beautiful
and its fruit looked delicious, and she wanted the wisdom it would
give her. So she took some of the fruit and ate it. Then she gave
some to her husband, who was with her, and he ate it, too. At that
moment their eyes were opened, and they suddenly felt shame
at their nakedness. So they sewed fig leaves together to cover
themselves."
—Genesis 3:1–7

A few weeks ago, my wife put an envelope with a check in our mailbox and stuck the little red flag up to alert the mail carrier that something was there to be picked up. A couple of days later, she received a call from one of our bank's branches. The banker told her a man was there, trying to cash a check she had written to him for a large amount. Could she verify it?

She was shocked! She said she had never heard of the person who was trying to cash her check. When the banker returned to confront the person, he ran away. We found out later that there are crooks out there who are able to wash the ink off of checks and write in whatever they want. We felt violated! Some crook was trying to take from us what didn't belong to him.

In a way, Adam and Eve violated God. They took from Him what did not belong to them. They took their God-given identity and the knowledge of good and evil that came from that origin and tried to make it their own!

"Then the LORD God said, 'Look, the human beings have become
like us, knowing both good and evil…'"
—Genesis 3:22

Reset Exercise: Recognize the Origin of Your Stolen Identity

Please write the name of God again in large block letters in your journal, but this time don't draw the first couple in the O of God. Instead, draw an arrow from the O of God to the outside. Draw the first couple standing *outside* God.

Now put a circle around Adam and Eve individually. You're going to need enough room so you can draw arrows in four directions from each of the circles:

The individual circles represent their new origin: themselves. The arrows represent the fact that they now view everyone and everything, including good and evil and right and wrong, from within themselves.

If you keep reading in Genesis—and I'd encourage you to read at least through chapter 11—you will see the beginning of the tragic effects of living life outside God, which extend to this very day.

What does this have to do with you? When Adam and Eve stepped away from God, they took all of us with them!

Bonhoeffer puts it like this: "As the image of God, man draws his life entirely from his origin in God, but the man who has become like God has forgotten how he was at his origin and has made himself his own creator and judge. What God had given man to be, man now desired to be through himself."[3]

I feel that, don't you? If we are honest with ourselves, don't we all want to be God? Don't you find yourself at least tempted to define good and evil, right and wrong, by your own understanding—and then apply it to others? Every day we judge people based on what *we* think is appropriate behavior. Even if you're a relativist who believes it is up to each person to decide what is right and wrong for yourself, what do you do when someone's right steps on your wrong? For example, the check thief! Maybe he's a Darwinist and believes in the survival of the fittest. He simply took our money to survive! Right and wrong can become very subjective, can't they? We all feel the symptoms of our first parents' choices.

How did Adam and Eve feel after taking what didn't belong to them?

"At that moment their eyes were opened and they suddenly felt shame at their nakedness. So they sewed fig leaves together to cover themselves."
—Genesis 3:7

When they looked at themselves, they didn't like what they saw. Why? God was missing! They only knew themselves now, and they felt ashamed, much the way you might have felt when your mom caught you with your hands in the forbidden cookie jar. Shame, says Bonhoeffer, is the inescapable remembrance that we have been estranged from God. Shame is a deep sense of loss that cannot be regained by any human effort.[4]

So, what did Adam and Eve do? They tried to cover up their nakedness in hopes of getting rid of their shame.

How did they cover up? You may be thinking, *Well, it says, "fig*

---

3. Bonhoeffer, *The Cost of Discipleship*, 22.
4. Ibid., 24.

leaves." That's true, but the real cover-up was *pride!*

They hid their culpability in pride. No one wanted to accept the blame for what had happened, so Adam and Eve pointed fingers at each other and the serpent. Adam even tried to blame God. He said, "It was the woman you gave me!" So all our troubles—personally, relationally, socially, and globally—result from trying to live from the origin of ourselves and according to the image pride creates. Pride determines winners and losers—who gets in and who has to stay out. Pride puts labels on others and propagates racism, abuse, and violence. Pride fosters materialism, jealousy, and division. Pride elevates some and shames others. We are cruel gods!

I know what you're thinking: *Hey, Dale, where's the hope you were talking about? This is getting depressing!*

Hope is on the way! Humanity may have abandoned God, but He never abandoned His creation! The story of the Bible is God's relentless pursuit to bring us back to Himself again—to offer His creation the opportunity to leave behind the cover-up of pride and step back into the O of God. That was Jesus's principal message. The Imago Dei can be restored!

How?

Jesus replied, "I tell you the truth, unless you are born again, you cannot see the Kingdom of God" (John 3:3).

How does one become born again? You have to take off your pride and receive the identity of God into your life. You have to give back to God His intellectual property, which is the knowledge of good and evil. The Bible calls this transaction *repentance.* The word literally means to turn around and walk a different way. It's what we saw the prodigal son do in chapter 4. He turned away from rebellion and returned home to his father. He never expected his father to take him back. He thought he had lost his identity as a son. But in the father's view, he had never stopped being a son! When he came home, his Abba embraced him as though he had never left!

As we come home to our Abba, through Jesus His Son, He gives us His Spirit. As we are reconnected to God the Father, the Spirit of God comes to indwell our lives. A spiritual reset begins to take place in our being, which will eventually be completed when we fully enter God's presence someday. The Bible affirms this truth in passages like this one:

"But whenever someone turns to the Lord, the veil is taken away. For the Lord is the Spirit, and wherever the Spirit of the Lord is, there is freedom. So all of us who have had that veil removed can see and reflect the glory of the Lord. And the Lord—who is the Spirit—makes us more and more like him as we are changed into his glorious image."
—2 Corinthians 3:16–18

That, in summary, is the creation, fall, and redemption story of Christianity.

And right here is where typical Christian teaching stops.

If we believe the story is true, then the Holy Spirit will automatically change us into God's image again. We expect that once we agree with the facts, our thought patterns, emotions, and behaviors will automatically change. Believe the truth, repent of your pride, and congratulations! Now the Holy Spirit will change you from the inside out, and you can live a perfect life.

How has that worked out for you? If I were reading this back when I was overwhelmed by panic attacks and intrusive thoughts, desperately trying to hold it together as a pastor, I can tell you what I'd be thinking: *I've heard all that a thousand times! I know what to believe. I just don't know* how *to believe it.*

As I said in chapter 2, we need to create new neural pathways for this new way of thinking. Until we leave what we've been used to, we cannot embrace what God has waiting for us.

Reset 12: Return to the Oasis of God

On my recent visit to the Middle East, I flew over portions of the wilderness through which God led His people on their journey from slavery in Egypt to the freedom of the Promised Land. In fact, years ago, I had the privilege of traveling in the wilderness by Jeep. It is a forbidding and hostile environment! It's what I imagine the landscape to be like on Mars.

In the wilderness, God's people had to learn to stop thinking like slaves and start thinking like the children of God. They had to rediscover who they were. God used the wilderness to help them do exactly that.

How? The same way He uses our "wilderness" experiences. For example, my wilderness experiences include my battle with my past and my struggles with mental illness. I've learned that instead of wandering in my wilderness, I can let God use those struggles to actually help me find myself and Him. That's what the wilderness provides: a place to find ourselves so that we can find God.

In the desert, one comes to the end of himself or herself. In Israel's case, the wilderness was the place where God met His people and where they learned total reliance on Him. That's what I mean when I say that in the wilderness, we find ourselves. All the crutches are gone. The distractions of life disappear. You're seemingly left alone; your sense of mortality becomes acute. Much that mattered before no longer holds value. All that matters is God. So, when you come to the end of yourself, you not only find yourself—more importantly, you find God. Suddenly, your wilderness becomes an oasis!

Let's get into the wilderness to discover our oasis.

Reset Exercise: Return to the Oasis of God: Morning Practice

I invite you to use this Reset exercise as a daily practice in the morning and the evening. Here are the guidelines for creating your oasis and the morning practice.

1. Begin by creating a circle that will become the wilderness you visit each day. I mean this quite literally. People who practice yoga haul their yoga mats to the gym, park, and on planes. Their yoga mat is their protected space where they meditate, stretch, pose, and sweat! You don't need a yoga mat, but you do need a defined space in the form of a circle.

Why a circle? It symbolizes the O of God from our earlier Reset exercise. We've come full circle (pardon the pun), and now, instead of Adam and Eve, I want you to literally put yourself in the O of God. Even if you're not sure you believe in God yet, this exercise will allow you to see and feel what finding your origin in God might be like, and who knows—you may even change your mind.

What I do know is changing the brain involves imagination!

When I was struggling as a child, I often used my imagination to escape reality, much like author James Thurber's fictional character Walter Mitty. But instead of using our imagination to escape reality, we're going to use it to enter reality. So, imagine the circle you are creating is the place where you will find your center in God.

The circle needs to be big enough for you to sit, stand, or even lay down in. You can create the boundaries from whatever material you want. You could cut a large piece of fabric or mat in the shape of a circle. If you're outside, you could draw a circle in the sand, or place some stones or sticks in the shape of an O. Whatever you do, make it visible, or it won't be effective.

2. Bring several items into your circle: index cards, a pen, a Bible, a piece of fruit, and your journal. Yes, I did say fruit—as in an apple, an orange, grapes, or any type of edible fruit you enjoy. One piece will do.

I invite you to step into the circle at least once a day, but preferably twice a day for the most benefit. If you practice this exercise twice a day, you will enter the circle in the morning before you begin the day and the evening as you end your day.

Let's try it right now! Make a circle using whatever is at hand to mark at least part of its circumference.

3. Once you're in the circle, the first thing I want you to do is to practice some breathing exercises to get still and focused. One very simple and effective breathing exercise I use is called the 4-7-8 relaxing breath exercise. I use it whenever I feel anxious, and it really is effective. Sit in your circle with your back straight. Place the tip of your tongue just behind your front teeth. You will keep your tongue there during the entire exercise. Now, exhale all the air in your lungs. Now close your mouth and inhale slowly through your nose to a mental count of four. Hold your breath for a mental count of seven. Exhale through your mouth and around your tongue for a count of eight. This is one breath. Do this sequence again three more times for a total of four breaths.

Did you try it? How did it feel? It may take some getting used to. The most important part is that exhaling should take twice as long as inhaling, so don't be as concerned about speed as keeping to the mental 4-7-8 count. With practice, you will learn to slow down your breath. You can do this breathing exercise as many times a day as you feel you need to, but always when you begin and leave your circle.

4. Now, let's do some decluttering! This is the stage in the "wilderness" when everything we depend on for our worth and everything we fear is put away. First, ask God verbally or silently to reveal to you anything or anyone you rely on other than Him to define your sense of worth, value, or identity. Your list may include things like these:

- Career
- Looks
- Grades
- Athletic abilities
- Parenting
- People pleasing
- Money
- Spirituality
- Good works
- Other people's opinions of you (by name)

God may reveal these things and people to you in thoughts or images. As you hear from God and write down what is revealed, place each index card outside the circle with a simple prayer: "God, I am giving _____ up to You. I will no longer allow it/him/her/them to define who I am or how I feel about myself."

At first, you may be disappointed to see how dependent your identity is on other people or circumstances, but don't worry; over time your identity will become less dependent on external things and you will eventually use fewer cards.

Our wilderness experiences can also be fraught with fear and worries. That has been my case since childhood. I've struggled with all kinds of fears, including the following:

- Being left alone
- Rejection (by God and others)
- Death
- Becoming financially poor
- Embarrassment
- Failure

What or whom are you afraid of? Ask God to reveal people, things, or issues that cause fear in your life. Just as you did with the people and things you use to define your worth, write each item individually on a card, place each card outside of the circle, and pray, "God, I am giving _____ up to You. I will no longer allow it/him/her/them to worry or frighten me."

I want you to focus less on how you feel as you do this exercise and more on just doing it. It has been said that feelings are wonderful servants but terrible masters. We are going to learn how not to let our feelings control our lives anymore! Agreed? You're not feeling it? Good! Just do it.

Congratulations! If you have done the above exercises, you are on the way to finding yourself. As you sit in your circle, everything that has defined your worth and value, and all your worries and fears, is now hopefully outside of you. Don't worry if you feel you have not completely cleaned house. That will come.

For now, where do these disciplines leave you? Look at your position. Where are you? In a circle? Not really. I want you to think of that circle as the O of God. Here are three ways to envision the O of God:

1. Know that you are in the center of God. You are inhabiting Him, and He is inhabiting you. This is an answer to one of Jesus's prayers:

"'I am praying not only for these disciples but also for all who will ever believe in me through their message. I pray that they will all be one, just as you and I are one—as you are in me, Father, and

I am in you. And may they be in us so that the world will believe
you sent me.'"
—John 17:23

"'When I am raised to life again, you will know that I am in my
Father, and you are in me, and I am in you.'"
—John 14:20

The back of our home has three large glass doors that face south. On sunny but frigid winter days, I love to sit in my reading chair and soak in the sun. It is so warm, and it helps me overcome the winter blues. A good dose of being in the sunshine does my soul well.

2. Soak in the presence of God by meditating on a few Scriptures. (See dalehummel.com for more Scriptures to use for daily meditation.) If you're in a place where you can read out loud, try speaking these verses so you can better focus your mind on the words and their meaning. Imagine you're practicing the 4-7-8 breathing exercise as you breathe in Scripture: as you read the verse(s), take them into your mind, hold the words there for a moment, and then, as though exhaling, try to feel (yes, feel) the meaning of the words. Try it:

"Consider the kind of extravagant love the Father has lavished
on us—He calls us children of God! It's true; we are His beloved
children. And in the same way the world didn't recognize Him, the
world does not recognize us either."
—1 John 3:1, The Voice

"My loved ones, we have been adopted into God's family; and
we are officially His children now. The full picture of our destiny is
not yet clear, but we know this much: when Jesus appears, we will
be like Him because we will see Him just as He is."
—1 John 3:2, The Voice, emphasis mine

Do you hear that? The Father loves you extravagantly. You

are His beloved child. It doesn't matter if no one else recognizes it; all that matters is that you know it. It's official: the adoption papers are signed by the ink of Christ's blood, proof that He gave up His life for you. Soak in the love of God; ask the Holy Spirit to wash you with this truth until it becomes a reality in you. Use your imagination; remember, it is a powerful tool God has given you.

Maybe, like me, you have used your imagination to escape reality and imagine being what you thought the world wanted you to be before you could feel accepted. No more fantasy! Use your God-given imagination to reset your thinking about yourself. Project the words you just read and thought about onto the screen in your mind. See God loving and accepting you just as you are, in whatever state you are in! In other words, you need to see that God loves you, even in your messiness, brokenness, doubts, and confusion. Even in unbelief!

This is the new reality that you will take with you when you leave the circle and head into your day. But don't leave yet. I want you to take something else with you.

3. Get out your piece of fruit! In Galatians 5, the apostle Paul describes nine facets of love, often referred to as the fruits of the Spirit. Here they are:

"But the Holy Spirit produces this kind of fruit in our lives: love, joy, peace, patience, kindness, goodness, faithfulness, gentleness, and self-control."
—Galatians 5:23

You cannot produce what you do not receive and what you do not enjoy! I want you to select just one facet (fruit) of love for today and read a verse or two that describes it. I'll select kindness. (Check out dalehummel.com, where I've given you several verses to go along with each fruit.)

"When God our Savior revealed his kindness and love, he saved us, not because of the righteous things we had done, but because

of his mercy. He washed away our sins, giving us a new birth and new life through the Holy Spirit. He generously poured out the Spirit upon us through Jesus Christ our Savior. Because of his grace he made us right in his sight and gave us confidence that we will inherit eternal life."
—*Titus 3:4–7*

What are some ways you have experienced the kindness of God? As you think about it, begin enjoying the fruit you brought with you into the circle. If it's really juicy, let it flow down your chin; enjoy the taste as you think about His kindness.

Here are some ways I've experienced God's kindness:

- Through the sacrifice of Jesus, who gave up His life freely for me
- In the fact that He has never abandoned me, despite all the difficulties I've endured, particularly in my childhood and my teenage years
- In being blessed with an incredible wife, children, and grandchildren
- In being allowed to serve great churches
- In the close friends He has surrounded me with through the years
- Through the blessing of good health
- In being able to come to terms with my struggles in the area of mental health
- In being surrounded with some great mental health professionals who have brought insight and meaning into my life
- In the flavor of chocolate–peanut butter ice cream!

Hey, kindness comes in all flavors!

I could go on, but you get the idea, right? As you finish your list of fruit, keep thinking of all the ways God has been kind to you.

Your circle time is nearly complete. In the resources available to you at dalehummel.com, I've laid out for you a way to listen and talk to God that is much more involved and can be included in your circle time with Him. But for now, complete your circle time with your 4-7-8 breathing exercise for a total of four breaths. As you do, concentrate on who you are in the Imago Dei. Enjoy all the fruit of God's kindness to you.

After you leave your circle, I have two very important practices for you to continue as you go through your day.

Reset Exercise: See the Good Fruit in Others

Now that you have received and enjoyed the fruit of kindness for yourself (or any fruit of the Spirit you choose), I want you to discipline your mind to look for ways that God reveals His kindness to you and others. This can be as simple as noticing someone opening the door for another. Look for kindness everywhere you go, and when you see it, celebrate it in your mind. Thank God for the kindness you see. If you see a person expressing kindness, say a silent prayer of blessing on him or her. If it's appropriate, tell that person you saw the act of kindness, and share how it blessed you.

For example, recently, my son-in-law rode his bike up a grueling climb to the top of Haleakala Volcano on the island of Maui. It was a strenuous climb of more than ten thousand feet! As he was nearing the top, his body was exhausted, and he didn't know if he would complete the ride. He prayed to God for help, and as he tells it, he "suddenly felt the push of wind, which seemed to carry me to the top." He finished his climb and collapsed on the ground. An older couple who had driven to the top were standing there and walked over to see if he was all right. He shared with them his achievement and God's goodness. They congratulated him, and the woman said, "You deserve some kind of recognition and award!" So she took off her tree of life necklace and placed it around his neck. It made his day!

Reset Exercise: Bless Others, and Bring Out Their Goodness

Here's the second thing I want you to practice today. Place a wreath of kindness figuratively around as many people as you can today through your own acts of kindness. You can express kindness through silent prayer, a smile, opening a door, an appropriate hug for someone you know, high fives, expressions of appreciation, or whatever you can do. Be sincere but intentional. I'm telling you, behaving this way will reset your mind and turn you into a different person!

Reset Exercise: Evening Practice

At the end of your day, lay out your circle, and enter it before turning in for the night. Do your 4-7-8 breathing for four breaths as you enter. While you're in the O of God, I want you to personalize and answer four questions:

1. *In the course of the day, did I take back anything I threw out of the circle today? For instance, did I allow someone at work or in the family to make me feel bad about myself?* If so, just pick up that index card (or create a new one, if you hadn't already created one) and toss it back out of the circle before you go to bed!
2. *Did I let pride get the best of me today? Did I find myself comparing, being jealous, putting others down, or gossiping?* Toss it out of the circle. You don't need to waste your energy by putting others down to feel better about yourself!
3. *What fears or worries crept back into my mind and tied up my emotions?* Name them, pick up the index cards (or create new ones if needed), and toss them out of the circle.
4. *Is there some sin, guilt, or shame I incurred today?* Confess it to the Creator, and receive His awaiting forgiveness. Toss the guilt, shame, and self-loathing out of the circle.

Use the rest of your circle time to savor the kindness you received, saw, and gave away. Eat another piece of fruit if it helps! Here's the key: end your day by resetting your mind into a positive and peaceful mode. I'll bet you will begin sleeping better and waking up with a more positive spirit, too!

The fruit of kindness is only the beginning. I've laid out a rhythm of nine days you can use to reset your mind and behavior (see dalehummel.com). Each day covers a different Scripture(s) that deals with identity, as well as a different fruit of the Spirit to focus on. I believe that within sixty days of daily discipline and practice, you will experience a noticeable difference in your thinking, feelings, and behavior.

Here's the real question: What are you going to do tomorrow? Are you willing to put the effort in? One Bible story that has always fascinated me occurs in John 5. Jesus encounters a man who had been an invalid for thirty-eight years. Upon seeing the crippled man, Jesus asks him, "Do you want to get well?" (John 5:6).

What a strange question! If you were an invalid for thirty-eight years of your life, wouldn't you want to be healed? Who would say, "No! I like being like this!"? But it happens. In my nearly forty years of ministry, I have met many who honestly don't want to be healed. They don't come out and say it, but their actions and attitudes prove it. Offered advice, given help and hope, they refuse to put the effort into new patterns of thinking and behavior. It can be easier to live in the deep rut of addiction, codependence, and self-pity than to change. I understand this; I'm often tempted myself to reach back and justify a negative outlook on life because of what happened to me in the past.

How about you? Do you want to be healed?

Let's do this together. It just takes a little faith!

Chapter 6
Reset Faith

T he moving truck was packed, and our car was full! We were heading west, all the way to the edge of the coast. I had finished seminary and said my good-byes to our little church out on the edge of town. Although it was hard to say farewell, especially to family, we knew deep down in our hearts that God had called us to a new and bigger challenge in the San Francisco Bay area.

As we traveled across the prairies and plains, I grew more excited as I thought about the prospects of leading a church twice the size of the one we left behind. The idea of moving from the rural Midwest to the cosmopolitan setting of the San Francisco Bay area was exhilarating.

But something terrible awaited me just a few hundred miles up the road. It happened as I began the ascent up the Rocky Mountains. I got bushwhacked! I can still picture the scene. Our vehicle was climbing up a steep grade. It was grey and damp outside, when suddenly, my soul was seized by the thought, *What if I fail?* I don't know why the idea hadn't occurred to me sooner! Then a whole avalanche of fearful thoughts tumbled into my mind:

- What if they don't like my preaching?
- What if the church of 240 declines instead of grows?
- What if we don't fit the fancy culture?
- What if…?

I felt like I did the day our firstborn was delivered. I remember standing in the labor and delivery room watching the doctor lift him up and hand him to my wife, whose tears of pain had turned into tears of joy. Mother and son were bonding, while I stared in shock. One thought headlined my frontal cortex: "What have I just done?" The fear of responsibility gripped and paralyzed me!

Have you ever had one of those soul-seizing, fear-gripping moments when you doubted yourself so much that you wished for a do-over—but it was too late?

That's how fear works, isn't it? It tries to keep you corralled in the familiar where life is safe and proven.

Back to my avalanche of fearful thoughts in the Rockies. I remember gripping the steering wheel, trying to stay focused on the winding road and dangerous curves, all while fighting a growing urge to turn around and go back to the dysfunction I had often complained about. That felt safe; this did not!

What about you? Maybe you are at a point in your life where you're wondering, *Can I really change? Maybe I need to simply accept the dysfunction and chaos in my life as my norm.* Perhaps you bought this book or someone gave it to you thinking that a journey towards a new mindset might help you, but now you're hesitating. Fear has ambushed you with doubt and discouragement. The committee in your mind is reminding you of all the books you've bought and read, the seminars and sermons you've heard, the counseling sessions you've been in, the prayers you've prayed, and the pills you've taken, but you've always ended up where you started. What if you fail again?

I want to share something with you that I heard God tell me on that mountain. I believe these words can give you the same hope and freedom they offered me. You may want to open your journal and write them down. I distinctly heard God say to me, "So what? What if you do fail? Just be faithful!"

Those words rushed into my mind and literally calmed the mental and emotional storm rocking my soul. I cannot explain the peace they brought over me, but as I summited the mountain, I can tell you I felt ready to head down the other side and embrace whatever lay ahead of me.

In this chapter, I want to encourage you not to give up. I want to share two powerful principles I've learned from the words I believe God gave me. After we look at those principles, I have an exercise I want you to practice that I believe will transform your thinking.

Reset 13: Defeat Your Fears by Calling Their Bluff

First, please write this statement down in your journal:

Reset #13: I can learn to defeat my fears by calling their bluff!

Having OCD has helped me learn how powerful this principle is! I've described in earlier chapters my struggle with ruminating thoughts, most of which are very negative in nature. Most of my thoughts are fear-based—fear of death and fear of all kinds of failure (spiritual, moral, financial, etc.). My fears are mostly irrational, yet they can be powerful and overwhelming.

When these fears occur, my common reaction is to fight them. I pray, I quote Scripture, I rebuke them, and I say all the right Christian phrases. Yet more often than not, all these efforts only make my fear(s) bigger instead of leaving me better. As you can imagine, it was a spiritually defeating and discouraging process—until about ten years ago, when my wise therapist, an expert on treating OCD, alerted me to a trick that deflates the debilitating ruminations. I remember sitting across from him when he spoke these eerily familiar words:

"*So what?* So what, Dale? So what if these irrational thoughts you're having actually happen? Embrace them, and they'll stop tormenting you."

So what? I'd heard that before—years before! God had actually given me a way to deal with fear, but it took me a long time to figure it out. The good news is, it works! I now have a weapon to use against my fearful thoughts.

By the way, researchers say that most of what we worry about never happens! Check the web: the statistics tell us between 85 and 99 percent of what we fear never takes place. Don't get hung up on what will most likely never happen!

How does this weapon work?

As I write this, I'm flying over Asia, where I've spoken at three conferences. I do a fair amount of overseas travel and ministry on behalf of our church. Our congregation has a huge and generous heart for planting churches among unreached people groups. I fly a lot, but I hate flying! It is like pouring gasoline on my OCD. *What if the pilots fall asleep? What if the ATC gives the wrong coordinates? What if the engines fail?*

I have a whole mental mantra I used to go through just to get on the plane. Once I was on board, I had other tortuous mental habits I'd have to perform, including praying a certain way for a certain amount of time to feel assured everything was going to be okay. I hated it but felt overwhelmingly compelled I had to do it or disaster would strike.

But now, when I sit on the plane and it begins to shake or make strange noises, and the fear of going down strikes, I just embrace it! I literally tell the fear, "You're right; we're probably going to crash, and I'm going to die or be severely injured, but my life insurance is paid up, and I know I'll be with Jesus, so bring it!" Sometimes I have to say it more than once, but it works. It's like I've called fear's bluff, and its attempt to defeat and lock my mind up fades away.

What irrational fears do you face? Try embracing them. Call their bluff.

Reset Exercise: Call Fear's Bluff

What are one or two fears you have been wrestling with? Go ahead and write them down. After you're done, underneath each fear write a positive statement that embraces the outcome you fear!

Here are two examples:

Fear: My throat has been hurting; do I have throat cancer?
Calling fear's bluff: I probably do have throat cancer and will die tomorrow. Bring it! I might as well eat that half-gallon of ice cream now!

Fear: What if my spouse is having an affair?
Calling fear's bluff: My spouse is probably having an affair, and our marriage is through! What shall I fix for dinner? Is this the night to put the trash out?

> Notice in my examples that I add something that mocks the fear or moves me on to what is normal, such as fixing dinner or taking out the trash.

Remember, most of our fears are irrational and will never be realized. I don't want you to think I don't take legitimate fears seriously; I do! But even then, we should not let them dominate or control our minds.

Reset 14: Believe the Spiritual Truth About Yourself

Let's look at a second powerful principle. On the mountain, I heard God telling me not only to call fear's bluff, but to move toward my destination by faith. What is faith?

"Faith is the assurance of things you have hoped for, the absolute conviction that there are realities you've never seen."
—Hebrews 11:1, The Voice

For me, the "realities" include mental and emotional wellness. I know that someday in God's presence (in what we think of as heaven), I will finally have complete and eternal peace of mind. But must it remain so elusive now? Is it something I have to die to experience? Or can the future be experienced in the present? Faith would seem to indicate so.

In his book *The Mysteries of the Kingdom*, Rabbi Jonathan Cahn shares some intriguing insights about the connection faith creates between the *here and now* and the *there and then*. In one of his excerpts titled "Living from the Future," he talks about the heaven and Earth continuum. I want to borrow and expand on a metaphor he creates.

Imagine there is an oasis with a grove of date palms, shade, and a fresh pool of water. It lies some distance in front of you. Meanwhile, you're standing in the hot sun in the middle of the desert. What do you want more than anything? To get to the oasis, to quench your thirst, and rest in the shade! Right? So where do you start? It seems obvious, doesn't it? You start where you are in the desert, and you move towards the oasis. But Cahn asks, "What if you set your heart on getting from there to here? What if you did it backward, proceeding not from the starting line, but from the finish line?"[1] Why not start from the oasis?

It sounds absurd, doesn't it? But is it? Jesus didn't seem to think so. In what we know as the Lord's prayer, He taught His followers to pray, "Thy will be done on earth as it is in heaven." Jesus called for living on earth as though you're living in heaven.

Is that truly possible? Let's look at a couple of verses from God's Word:

"But God is so rich in mercy, and he loved us so much, that even though we were dead because of our sins, he gave us life when he raised Christ from the dead. (It is only by God's grace that you have been saved!) For he raised us from the dead along with Christ and seated us with him in the heavenly realms because we are united with Christ Jesus."
—Ephesians 2:4–6

"Since you have been raised to new life with Christ, set your sights on the realities of heaven, where Christ sits in the place of honor at God's right hand. Think about the things of heaven, not the things of earth. For you died to this life, and your real life is hidden with Christ in God."
—Colossians 3:1–3

In these letters, Paul seems to be challenging the followers of Jesus to change their perspective, the lens through which they view themselves and life around them. In other words, I can see myself in my present circumstances, or I can choose by faith to see myself in my future reality within my present circumstances!

Let's talk astronomy for a moment. According to the website Space Today, "The star Polaris, which we refer to as the North Star or North Pole Star, is 680 lightyears away. The light takes 680 years to travel to Earth, so it is 680 years old when we see it."[2]

When I see the light from the North Star, I am actually looking 680 years into the past! I don't even think about the faith it takes to believe that because we know the physics concerning the speed of light. But it

1. Jonathan Cahn, *The Book of Mysteries* (Lake Mary, Florida: Charisma Media, 2018), 301.
2. "Q 'n A: Answers to Your Questions," Space Today, http://www.spacetoday.org/Questions/StarlightAge.html.

is cool to think that you can see the past as if it were the present.

Here's my point: Why would we doubt that we cannot see the future, too? It just depends on where we choose to start.

How do we live out of our assured and completed future? What evidence do we have that it's possible?

Cahn has another chapter in his book titled *The Power of As*.[3] In it, he mentions Ephesians 5:1: "Therefore be imitators of God, as beloved children."

What does it mean to be an imitator of God as a beloved child? Paul employs a Greek word transliterated as *hoce*, which can be translated as "the same way as, or just like." In that case, it would read, "Be imitators of God in the same way as, or just like, beloved children." Cahn says, "In order to live like beloved children you have to know what beloved children are like, how they behave, then you can live as though you're one of them. In God you have the power to live…as you are yet to be."[4]

A great illustration of this is found in the Old Testament book of Judges, chapter 6. The story is about a man named Gideon. God appeared to him and gave him specific directions to save Israel from their enemies. Here's how the angel addressed Gideon: "The angel of the Lord appeared to him and said, 'Mighty hero, the Lord is with you'" (Jud. 6:12).

But there's one problem: Gideon is a coward! Nevertheless, God saw past his cowardice. He saw the potential in Gideon and, in essence, told him to start acting like he was to become! In other words, start from the finish line! See yourself as God sees you, complete in Christ, and then act from that position, not from the position of defeat.

The story of David and Goliath is another powerful reminder of choosing which position we are going to live out of. In 1 Samuel, we learn that the Israelites and their king are living in defeat. They are afraid of the Philistines' secret weapon, the giant named Goliath. They are paralyzed with fear. But when young David the shepherd boy comes to visit the war front with some supplies for his brothers and sees the giant's size and hears his taunts, David does not back down. He claims victory before the battle is fought. That's because he was already living the victory!

3. Cahn, *The Book of Mysteries*, 258.
4. Ibid.

Faith, then, is tapping into what Christ has already completed for each of us. It is mentally, emotionally, and spiritually living from another realm while living here!

Here's the big question: How do you put that spiritual idea into practice? How do you begin at the end?

In the chapter on identity, I taught you how to reclaim your self-image by living in the O of God. I encouraged you to daily create a circle that represents God's presence, enter the circle, and learn to be with God. I gave you several practical exercises, which were meant to help you declutter your life and surrender yourself completely to the presence of God. I challenged you to choose one of the nine characteristics of Christ's character to internalize and manifest toward others, such as kindness.

I want to help you take that to a more advanced level with this next simple exercise of faith.

Reset Exercise: Believe You Are Already Perfect in Christ

Before you leave your next circle time with God, think about the fruit you chose to enjoy (see page 95). Let's suppose you chose the fruit of patience. Aren't you brave? This exercise is not about becoming patient, but believing that you already are patient in Christ. Therefore, you're not spiritually starting from where you are presently. You are switching perspectives and looking through the lens of where you are spiritually (seated with Christ in the heavenlies).

Using the 4-7-8 breathing technique I taught you (see page 91), do a cycle of three breaths while focusing on the reality that you are already patient in Christ. Accept this as truth. You are living on a higher plane in Christ. This is your destiny in Christ Jesus, and by faith, you have arrived there.

I want you to engage your wonderful God-given imagination now. This is one of the ways you change your brain. As you've learned in previous chapters, the imagination is powerful. We can raise and lower our blood pressure based on the way we use our imagination. We can convince our brain that a spider is crawling up our leg and actually feel like it's happening, to the point we will reach down to smack it! So take that God-given gift of your imagination and enter what you believe will be your first event of the day.

For example, my first challenge will be traffic! There is a series of at least seven stoplights between my house and work. They are stretched out far enough that I can actually get up to 60 mph between them. But invariably, I never make the green lights! I'll get up to speed and then have to slow down and stop—and often it's because someone ahead of me is going too slow. Wow, I'm feeling angry and impatient just typing this!

So, in my circle time with God, I visualize myself in the car at each of the lights. By faith, I see myself in the future! But instead of feeling angry and impatient, trying to jockey for position, I imagine Christ's Spirit in me. I see His patience in my mind's eye. He is far less concerned about making all the green lights. He savors the moments to stop. He looks around at those ahead, beside, and behind Him, and He thinks about who they are and what their lives must be like. Because patience is an attribute of love, He uses the time spent at the stoplights to pray for them, bringing them before His Father, asking His Abba to bless them.

Patience is the practice of putting others first, even when it inconveniences us. In Christ, we learn that there's no such thing as inconvenience. Everything is an opportunity.

As fear strikes me with the thought that I'll be late if I don't push the pedal to the floor as though I'm in a Mario Kart video game, I call fear's bluff: "I probably will be late! I may even get fired. Well, then I won't have to worry about any more traffic. Bring it!"

Proceed through the rest of the expected events of your day, as much as time allows.

What have we done in that exercise? We have premeditated our encounters. We have lived them in the future, and we have experienced them by faith out of a lens of victory rather than defeat!

You may not have the time to premeditate your whole day at once, but you can focus victoriously in faith from event to event. Once you get used to this practice, you can do it in the car before you go into the office, at your desk before you go into a meeting, or in your van before the kids come piling in from a full day at school.

As you become more discerning, you will be able to call on different attributes of Christ, depending on the challenge or opportunity you anticipate facing. You are resetting your brain by faith. You are living in heaven on Earth.

Chapter 7
Reset Community

Over the past few years, I have become very interested in the reports of visions, dreams, and miracles. Because our church is quite involved in overseas ministry in some of the most challenging places on Earth, I set out to meet a few of our trusted partners to get firsthand evidence and stories of God's mighty movement in these regions.

What I did not expect was to personally experience a miracle that was repeated in all three places. Let me tell you about it.

My first stop was in Asia. I cannot tell you where or give you many details, as those who minister there are always in danger of being arrested or losing their lives. I spent most of my time with two key leaders and then was introduced to others who were part of this unique movement of God. I heard stories and met people who had received visions of Christ and experienced miraculous healing.

But what struck me was the deep sense of community I experienced while I was with these leaders. In a strange way, I felt like I was home. I felt like I belonged. I wanted to stay, despite the danger. Being part of this community seemed worth the risk. When I left, I felt like I was leaving the warmth of a home and walking into the cold of winter. What happened in Asia?

Whatever it was, it happened again six weeks later, when I traveled to the West Coast of the United States. I had been put in touch with two men who had been part of the beginning of the Jesus People movement, as well as the start of the Vineyard movement. We had never met before. My goal was to hear how God moved in those early days of two great spiritual outbreaks.

Their recollection of the scores of changed lives and miracles were powerful and moving. But what happened in our meeting was more profound than anything they told me. I felt it again! The same experience I had in Asia was happening in the house where we had gathered. Once again, I felt like I had become a part of a deep fellowship. I didn't want to leave!

Then I made another journey, this time to the Middle East. Again, I cannot be specific because of the vulnerability of those who minister in the region. I was fortunate to have my wife with me on this trip. We met refugees our church has been helping with food, clothing, and education. We then spent some significant time with about thirty partners who serve throughout the Middle East in various vocations. Each of them has been through a one-year cohort experience to prepare them for the challenges they will face in their country.

As we listened to each of their stories and heard about visions, dreams, and miracles, we felt ourselves transported into a different atmosphere. I was experiencing the same thing I did in Asia. Our time ended with the group surrounding my wife and me, praying over some burdens we've been carrying for quite some time. It was a profound moment for us, and now, three months later, God is miraculously moving in the particular situation they prayed for!

Three totally different contexts, but the same vibe! What was I experiencing? Some things are hard to put into words. But I'll try.

Reset 15: Identify What You Want in Community with Others

Below, I share what happened to me, and what my wife also experienced with me in the Middle East, in six general categories. I encourage you to take out a pen and circle the attributes you wish you could encounter on a regular basis in community with others.

1. Genuineness

I'll be up-front and tell you that I have a tendency to question people's genuineness. I suppose my past has something to do with that. It seemed that whenever people were nice to me, they expected to receive something in return. In all three venues I experienced, no one wanted anything. They were simply interested in me.

We live in such a fake world. There's fake news, fake appearances, fake relationships, fake food, fake hair, fake accessories, and fake attempts at appearing to really care and be concerned. It's hard to know what's real anymore, but when you really experience the authentic, it is powerful! What I experienced in all three settings was sincere. It was real! I didn't sense pride, jealousy, or competition.

2. Joy

One of the groups has experienced a lot of persecution. A member of that community told us that he has repeatedly received death threats and continually has to watch his back. He's had many instances of being surrounded by enemies threatening to kill him. Despite the continual threats and persecution, he speaks with a smile on his face and a peace that transcends his circumstances. There is genuine joy in his life.

Joy is different than happiness. It has been said that *happiness* is based on our happenings, so it fluctuates according to your circumstances. However, *joy* is something you have or experience no matter what your circumstances. Our friends in Asia and the Middle East live in challenging situations. Life is hard and sometimes very lonely. Yet despite the difficulties, they seem to have matured to a place of steady joy. Don't get me wrong, they have their moments—but generally speaking, joy has taken over their attitudes. Self-pity is absent!

3. Love

I personally know a member of a community who converted to Christ by hearing a radio broadcast of the Good News of Jesus's love for the world. When she announced her conversion, she was threatened and told that if she did not recant, she would be kicked out of her family and village. Her faith, though new, was strong. So her brother beat her in front of the family and villagers. Barely able to walk, she left the community, but as soon as she was healed, she went back to tell her family and villagers about the love of God. Again, she was severely beaten and had her hair pulled out.

This happened yet another time, until finally, her family realized something very real and powerful had happened to her. How could she love them when they were treating her so badly? They received her back, and eventually, her sisters and the brother who beat her gave their lives to Christ. She is one of the most amazing people I've ever met. She belongs to the ranks of the apostles! What inspires love like this?

The entertainer Tina Turner sang, "What's love got to do with it?" The answer is, a lot! But what is love? Is it physical, sensual, or magical? Is love something you fall into and fall out of? Is love conditional? True love is not any of those things. True love has no sense of itself; it is only aware of the other. That means true love is as much an act of the will as it is the heart.

As I listened to the stories of the communities in Asia, the Middle East, and the West Coast, I heard about the struggle to love enemies, to love those who put you down, or want you to leave, or dislike how you dress or look. It isn't easy. There was hurt and frustration, but also perseverance. Those we were with had broken through to say they genuinely loved those who opposed them. The love was apparent; we felt it.

4. Vulnerability

Another quality I noticed in each of the groups I/we met with was a deep level of openness. Several group members shared how difficult it was to move overseas and settle into hostile environments. They talked about their fears and insecurities and how they had to learn to depend on God and trust in each other. Some shared how, at times, they struggled with not being near family.

I hate feeling vulnerable. I suppose a lot of that has to do with my childhood abuse. I am always on guard. I struggle to trust people. I constantly question motives. It's so unhealthy to live that way. To experience genuineness, joy, and love, one must become vulnerable. To do so requires the courage to trust, knowing you could get burned. As I listened to all three communities of faith, I found people who risked being vulnerable because the possibility of genuine, joyful, loving community was worth it!

They didn't even know us, even though we directly support some of them! Yet all three groups poured out their hearts in transparency. They were not afraid to be themselves. There were no hushed tones or wary looks, and their arms were not folded in defense. There was nothing to hide from each other. We could tell they felt safe within the fellowship.

5. Forgiveness

I asked various members of the communities we visited how they handled disagreements among themselves. One of the groups spoke of the challenges of being on teams with people who do things differently or who struggle at times with negative attitudes and disagreements. They admitted that such negativity can quickly ruin a team. When those you're trying to minister to see this negativity, the whole team loses credibility. So forgiveness becomes very important.

The groups shared that they have had to learn how to listen to each other when grievances are committed. This leads to a covenant to confess sins committed against individuals and the community. The response must always be forgiveness. It is never an option! When someone says they're sorry, it is time to forgive and move on. Jesus never held grudges; therefore, we shouldn't either.

6. Worship

Finally, they love to worship. In one of the settings, a member pulled out a guitar and began to spontaneously sing songs to the Lord. As I watched, I was moved by how abandoned the members of the group were in worshipping Jesus. I felt convicted. Many times, I just mouth lyrics or prayers without really experiencing what I'm saying. But their depth of love for Jesus swept over me.

In all three environments, I also noticed there was a preoccupation with Jesus. Everyone's words pointed toward Him because they felt they had received so much from Him. Jesus was clearly their reference point for their actions and attitudes. Worship in this context was about self-sacrifice.

Genuineness, joy, love, vulnerability, forgiveness, and worship were the qualities that captured my mind and heart and made me want to stay. How many of the six characteristics that I mentioned did you circle? All six? I hope so. Wouldn't you want to be a part of a community that practiced these attitudes on a consistent basis?

Reset 16: Create the Environment for Genuine Community

Just like our minds need a reset, our community also needs a reset.

Dietrich Bonhoeffer, the Lutheran pastor and theologian killed by the Nazis during World War II, wrote a little book titled *Life Together*. In it, he outlines what leads to true life-transforming community. When I came home from my journeys, I pulled out the book and decided to reread it. In its pages, I found the secrets behind the manifestations of grace I had experienced in those special gatherings.

I realize that you might not ascribe to the Christian faith. I still want to encourage you to keep reading. Perhaps seeing how true followers of Jesus are supposed to live will inspire you to consider the claims of Christ and to seek out an authentic Christian community. Will you at least consider it?

Bonhoeffer says that true, deep community is based on who Jesus is. Those who gather together do so around Jesus and what He has done for them. Authentic Christian community takes its identity from being in Christ.

In the chapter on identity, we discovered the importance of entering into the "O" of God—that is, letting Him define our sense of being, worth, and value. Because we find in Christ all we need, we do not necessarily look to the other members of the community for what is lacking in our lives. In other words, because Christ saves me from my sin, I do not need to look for rescue anywhere else. Because He justifies me, I don't need to try to justify myself or get another person to validate my existence, worth, or value. Because Jesus declares me righteous apart from any effort of my own, I don't need to compare myself to anyone to feel good enough.[1]

So, why do we need community?

Bonhoeffer says, "The Christian needs another Christian who speaks God's word to them."[2] They need their brother or sister in Christ to speak God's truth about them. During times of discouragement and uncertainty, which we all face, we need someone in our lives who represents Jesus to tell us we are loved, forgiven, accepted, and full of worth. In other words, we need to be Jesus to each other to help each other be like Jesus!

Later in the book, Bonhoeffer shares six ministries, or personal disciplines, that are necessary for creating the kind of healing community I encountered. I have added a seventh one—the ministry of thankfulness. Let's explore these important disciplines.

1. The Ministry of Holding One's Tongue

Boy, that's convicting, isn't it? Bonhoeffer says, "Often we combat

---

1. Bonhoeffer, *Life Together*, 22.
2. Ibid., 23.

our evil thoughts most effectively if we absolutely refuse to allow them to be expressed in words!"[3] Amen to that! Sounds like it should be so easy, but it's not! Why not? Because most of the time, when we want to give someone a "piece of our mind," it's to feel better about ourselves! To prove that we were right and they were wrong, to hand down judgment! Bonhoeffer suggests that the only time we should ever speak our evil thoughts is in confession to God as we seek His forgiveness!

James the Apostle wrote, "For we all stumble in many ways. If anyone does not stumble in what he says, he is a perfect man, able to bridle the whole body as well" (James 3:2, NASB).

Because none of us is perfect, that means we have to practice holding our tongues on a daily basis!

Reset Exercise: Hold Your Tongue

In your own circle time with God, make it a daily prayer and a conscious habit to replace every nasty thing you want to tell someone with an opposite word of praise. This forces you to look for the good in them rather than obsessing on the meanness or evil you see in them. What you will soon discover if you do this is that you can actually begin to change their behavior.

An added bonus: You are also resetting your own mind!

2. The Ministry of Meekness

Bonhoeffer plainly says that to become servants, we must first practice thinking little of ourselves.[4] When I think about that, it strikes me in two ways. First, I need to spend less time thinking about myself. Second, I need to think little enough of myself so I can put others above me!

Now, let me give you a twist on this: you may actually need to think *bigger* about yourself. A lot of us, because of our background and emotional baggage, may actually hate ourselves. I have struggled with this throughout my life because of my past. I've never felt good enough

---

3. Ibid., 92.
4. Ibid., 94.

for God or good enough for others. When I discovered my identity in Christ, and my self-image began to heal, then I began to understand what humility really means.

Humility means embracing God's love for me. When I do that, it's easier to love others and put them first. So the solution to thinking less of yourself and thinking more of yourself is the same: stop seeking honor from others, and accept the honor of God's grace demonstrated toward you in Christ Jesus.

I like the way this Scripture is worded:

> "'That's why it is hard to see how true faith is even possible for
> you: you are consumed by the approval of other men, longing to
> look good in their eyes; and yet you disregard the approval of the
> one true God.'"
> —John 5:44, The Voice

When I don't need anyone else's approval, I'm able to minister and love them with no strings attached.

Begin looking for simple ways to honor others by writing encouraging notes. Be specific about what you see in them that reflects something of the image of God. Don't put your name on the note. Do this weekly, and it will become a habit of life. Not only are you changing your community, you are changing how you think!

3. The Ministry of Listening

That is a gift for sure, isn't it? Whom do you wish would listen to you more? A spouse? A child? A friend? A boss or coworker? We all want to be listened to. Did you know that in communication, the average delay between when someone speaks to you and you respond is a whopping half of a second? How can anyone really be listening when they fire back in half of a second?

Bonhoeffer writes, "The first service that one owes to others in the fellowship consists in listening to them. Just as love to God begins with listening to His Word, so the beginning of love for [others in community] is learning to listen to them."[5]

---

5. Ibid., 97.

"Understand this, my dear brothers and sisters: You must all be quick to listen, slow to speak, and slow to get angry."
—James 1:19

Here is an exercise that will improve your listening skill. We will call it the three-second rule. Practice waiting three seconds before responding to people who are talking to you. Just count it off in your mind: "One one thousand, two one thousand, three one thousand," and *then* speak. When they notice you taking your time to answer and ask you why, just tell them, "I'm working on being a better listener so that you feel heard!" Count how long it takes them to know what to say when you tell them that!

4. *The Ministry of Helpfulness*

Bonhoeffer says that *active helpfulness* is necessary in authentic Christian community. Active helpfulness is just like it sounds. He means always being on the lookout for how one can help the other person, no matter how small the task. In Christian community, there is never any helpfulness that is too big or too small.

The sincere ministry of helpfulness is not dependent on convenience. If you read the Gospels carefully, you will note that Jesus was continuously being interrupted by the needs of others. When He had to deal with some really bad news about the death of his cousin, John the Baptist, He isolated Himself: "As soon as Jesus heard the news, he left in a boat to a remote area to be alone" (Matt. 14:13).

Even Jesus needed alone time to collect His thoughts and emotions and talk to His Father. But the crowds followed Him. When He stepped off the boat, Matthew 14:14 says, "Jesus saw the huge crowd as he stepped from the boat, and he had compassion on them and healed their sick."

He didn't grimace, get angry, or roll His eyes. Despite being weary and sad, His love for the people compelled Him to keep giving. If you keep reading Matthew 14, you'll discover that Jesus even fed the crowd of five thousand!

I'm not suggesting you invite the whole neighborhood over and try to feed them, but you could begin looking for simple ways to be more helpful at home, work, school, or wherever you land each day. Here are some ideas:

- Pick up around the house without being asked.
- Take over doing dishes for the night if you live with someone.
- Hold doors open for people, and let them go ahead of you.
- Empty the trash at work so the custodian doesn't have to.
- Assist coworkers with menial tasks so they can get done sooner.
- Shovel the neighbors' drive if you live where it snows.

What are some other ways you can practice active helpfulness?

5. The Ministry of Bearing

Paul wrote the followers of Jesus in Galatia these words: "Share each other's burdens, and in this way obey the law of Christ" (Gal. 6:2).

To bear the burden of others means more than helping them with some project or sympathizing with them in their grief or pain. To *bear* means to suffer and endure another person. Isn't that what Jesus did on the cross? Isaiah 53:4–5 says, "Yet it was our weaknesses he carried; it was our sorrows that weighed him down. And we thought his troubles were a punishment from God, a punishment for his own sins! But he was pierced for our rebellion, crushed for our sins. He was beaten so we could be whole. He was whipped so we could be healed."

Jesus carried the weight of our weaknesses. He bore the burden of our troubles. Why? Because He genuinely loves us.

My wife and I have been praying quite earnestly for the past several years about a situation involving a person we love and care about. Recently, I complained to God that I wasn't seeing any evidence He was at work in the person's life. Within a week of asking God for some indication that He was at work, I received communication from the individual. I found out that he was struggling and looking for a place to land. He was out of money, out of a job, and had some big medical needs. He didn't ask, but the Holy Spirit prompted me that we should open our home to him.

Have you ever argued with God? I did. I was thankful this person's life seemed to be turning a corner and he was willing to receive help, but I was very unsure about the interruption to my already stressful life. Did I want to bear the presence of his dogs (I have allergies), the disruptions to our routine, the added costs—not to mention temperament and attitude? The plain truth was *no!*

Then the Lord convicted me with a question: "Why did you ask for evidence if you're not willing to help be the solution?"

He had me! I stood down and told the Lord that despite the burden to bear, I would do it in the spirit of Christ, but I would need all His help. How could I not do for another what Christ did for me?

In genuine community, we don't put up with each other; we learn to bear one another's burdens, whatever they might be. Don't get me wrong—I am not talking about enabling people's bad behavior. There's a difference between bearing another's burden and enabling them to continue behaving badly. Bearing a burden means patiently and lovingly working with a person toward healing and wholeness. Sometimes, that requires godly confrontation toward a good end.

Whose burden(s) do you need to learn to bear?

6. The Ministry of Proclaiming

What Bonhoeffer means by that is the ministry of speaking God's truth to one another in community. I found this practiced consistently among those I visited in Asia, the Middle East and on the west coast. Their conversations were laced with Scripture, if not direct quotes then they paraphrased versions God's truth. They spoke these words freely, lovingly but with the authority of "but here's what God says…"

Bonhoeffer writes, "Nothing can be more cruel than the tenderness that consigns another to his sin. Nothing can be more compassionate than the severe rebuke that calls a brother back from the path."[6]

There is joy in community when we can declare God's word as a blessing on another person's life. There is fear when we sense we may need to speak God's word as measure of correction. I have had to do this many times. The posture I have learned to take is found in Galatians 6:1. The Voice Translation puts the verse like this: "My spiritual brothers and sisters, if one of our faithful has fallen into a trap and is snared by sin, don't stand idle and watch his demise. Gently restore him, being careful not to step into your own snare."

This is very difficult to do when you are not in relationship with the person. However, when friendship has developed and trust has been built, it is much easier because at least the person knows your heart. People you become friends with may balk at first when you try to correct

---

6. Ibid., 107.

them, but as the rest of the community shares the same sentiments of correction, it is often successful. Later, they often express thankfulness.

Let me share one more ministry, which I have added to Bonhoeffer's list.

7. The Ministry of Thankfulness

For the past several years, I have begun each day, as soon as I get out of bed, by thanking God for at least five people or situations. I do this to combat all the negative thoughts, worries, and responsibilities that present themselves at the threshold of a new day.

The practice helps rewire my brain for the day. Developing a thankful spirit helps me see the good in others and even in difficult circumstances. As we have learned, part of retraining the brain is the repetitive practice of new behavior until it becomes our new default for living. The Apostle Paul wrote to a community of believers living in Thessaloniki these words: "Be thankful in all circumstances, for this is God's will for you who belong to Christ Jesus" (1 Thess. 5:18).

Would you be willing to start your day, every day, by thanking God for five people or things in your life? Would you join me in keeping that thankful spirit alive throughout the day so that even when you meet difficult people or situations, you try to find something to be thankful for?

This brings us to a challenge! It is one thing to try to change our thinking and practice all these helpful steps in our relationships. And it's true that as we change ourselves, others around us may change as well. But what about a consistent and trusted community who can provide these ministries to *you?* Do you have a group of people in your life with whom you meet regularly for close fellowship? If you do, is it a group that you feel is tightly knit together and where you can be yourself, be accepted, loved, and encouraged?

My vision for you is that you could find or begin a Reset Community in which the principles in this book could be shared and practiced. I want you to have a gathering of like-spirited people who are all pulling in the same direction, a place that feels like home, safe and filled with hope.

I believe that such a group is necessary to experience the healing that God wants for your soul. That's what drew me to the three groups I was part of this past year. There was an unusual sense of healing in the atmosphere. I felt totally at peace. I had found a place where I could simply be loved, accepted, forgiven, encouraged, helped, corrected, directed, and motivated. I found it interesting that as I talked to the groups, I discovered what I thought was unusual and profound was normal to them: "We hear it all the time from people who visit or join us, but to us it's just how we do life. It is what we strive for. Do we fail sometimes? Of course but there are enough of us to pick the other up and continue the journey together."

So, what can you do to begin your journey toward greater mental and emotional healing? Well, you've already taken the first step of reading this book and beginning to practice the exercises. You are already beginning to reset your mind and retrain your brain!

What are some of the differences you are noticing? What have others noticed about you? My wife has often commented about the things she has seen changing in me. That is so helpful to hear, and it encourages me to continue.

As a next step, consider forming your own Reset Community.

Reset Exercise: Form a New Community

Is there someone you know who you think might benefit from forming a Reset Community with you? Make a potential list right now in your Reset Journal of the people you think could benefit from being in community with you.

If you're so inclined, pray over the list and ask God to help direct you to the people you should ask. Meet one-on-one over coffee and tell the person how this book and its principles and practices are changing your life. When you engage the people on your list, ask them if they would be willing to read the book with you and meet once a week to simply exchange what you're both discovering. As you each read the last chapter on community, ask them if they would like to continue with you in forming a close gathering that meets regularly for friendship, prayer, healing, and hope.

Use the headings of this chapter to serve as a charter for how your Reset Group might function. In other words, aim to be a community where together, you practice exhibiting the following characteristics:

- Genuine
- Joyful
- Loving
- Vulnerable
- Forgiving
- Worshipful

If you are not a person of faith, you can leave "worshipful" as an option. If you are a follower of Christ with a friend you would like to invite into community who may not ascribe to Christianity, that's okay. Give them a copy of the book to read first. You may find that they are willing to be a part of the group, as long as they don't feel pressure to convert! Don't try to convert them; let them simply experience God working in and through them and let them decide with God's help. Focus your attention on learning to love them unconditionally, as God does each one of us.

As you describe the aim of your Reset Community, agree to the seven attitudes that Dietrich Bonhoeffer described as ministries within the community:

- The ministry of holding one's tongue
- The ministry of meekness
- The ministry of listening
- The ministry of helpfulness
- The ministry of bearing
- The ministry of proclaiming
- The ministry of thankfulness

My suggestion is, when two or more of you agree on what you want your Reset Community to become, also agree on the seven attitudes you will seek to practice. I believe the next steps would be to use the chapters of this book as a basis for your discussions. Before doing so, have each person agree to the following guidelines:

1. I/we agree to review the aim and attitudes of our Reset Group at the beginning of each meeting.

2. I/we agree to ask the group members if they feel we are making progress in living out the aim and attitudes of our Reset Group.
3. I/we agree to respect each other's information and keep what is shared in the group in the strictest confidentiality.
4. I/we agree to attend every session, barring any emergencies.
5. I/we agree that our purpose is not to fix each other but to listen, encourage, and help only when members of the group ask for it.

Here's a suggested format you may want to follow. It is important that you do not hurry through this. Feel free to adjust the sessions to fit your needs as a group.

Week 1: Briefly discuss my story and how you can relate to it. Take the time to talk about your own story. I suggest you limit each person's time of sharing to no more than ten minutes. It is important that each group member shares his or her story.

Week 2: Discuss what you learned about the mind and the brain. How has the human condition of sin affected your mindset?

Week 3: Discuss how neuroplasticity can reset your thinking. Include discussion on the importance of thoughts, images, and ideas.

Week 4: Discuss chapter 3 of the book.

Weeks 5 and 6: Discuss chapter 4.

Week 7: Discuss chapter 5.

Week 8: Discuss chapter 6.

Week 9: Discuss chapter 7.

Dear friend, I pray that reading this book has given you a renewed sense of hope. I believe that if you will take the principles in each chapter and sincerely apply them to your life, you will reset your thinking! You will begin to live every day like it's a new day. A healthier future is just around the corner. Though it is often said that God loves you, I want you to know that He really does. He cares about your personal story. He proved it by giving the life of His Son Jesus Christ to die your death so you can live His life.

Reset is all about actualizing what He has made possible for you and me. I should know—it is happening to me! If God can transform my thinking and my living, He can do it for you as well.

Reset Statements and Exercises

To facilitate individual or group study, I have repeated the Reset statements and exercises from this book here, all in one place.

Reset 1: Acknowledge That God Chose You
Reset 2: Focus on God's Purpose for Your Life
Reset 3: Surrender to the Spirit within You

Reset Exercise: Surrender to the Spirit, Part 1

I'd like to invite you to try an exercise. If you're not sitting down right now, find a place where you can rest your weight. Take a few deep, cleansing breaths and center yourself.

Begin by focusing on the fact that you are resting all your weight on whatever object you're sitting on. That chair, couch, or stool is bearing you up. I doubt very much you're worried about whether it can bear your weight. You have simply transferred your trust to it.

Now, close your eyes and become aware that you're resting the weight of your life on whatever object you are sitting on. When you're focused, then resume reading.

Reset Exercise: Surrender to the Spirit, Part 2

Close your eyes again, and try to see yourself fully transferring the weight of your life to the Holy Spirit. It may be helpful to do some deep breathing, just like a trainer or class leader encourages you to do when you're exercising. With each exhale, surrender more and more to the Spirit until you feel like everything your soul has been carrying is now on Him.

Set the book down, and try the exercise again. Take your time. It might be awkward at first, much like learning to stand on a Bosu ball in the gym. But with practice, it will become natural.

Reset Exercise: Visualize Living in the Image of God

Read the statement you wrote in your journal:

God has chosen me unconditionally for the purpose of being transformed into the image of His Son through the continual presence and power of the Holy Spirit whom I am learning to rest in.

Remembering the power of images, can you visualize a picture of what this looks like for you? Try your hand at a bit of art. In your journal, underneath what you wrote, sketch out a scene or a symbol that represents what you just put in print.

If you feel secure enough to share what you drew with someone who will receive you with love and acceptance, tell them what it means to you.

Reset 4: Understand That God Is Very Fond of You
Reset 5: Focus on Seeing Heaven on Earth

Reset Exercise: Visualize Your Attitude

Take a few minutes to think about how you're feeling about your life right now. What word(s) come to mind? If you were an artist, how would you visually represent your attitude?

Please open your journal and put your thoughts down in words. Leave some space, and then draw the image you have in your mind about how you're feeling.

For example, you might describe your attitude by simply writing down the word "Happy." A smiley face may be all you need to represent your present state of being. Or you may come up with something more descriptive. Maybe you're feeling very inferior today, so you scribble down "Inferior!" You could draw yourself as a child, standing in the shadow of a tall, menacing giant.

Try your hand at describing and drawing what's going on in your mind and heart right now.

Reset 6: Become Willing to Receive Forgiveness

Reset Exercise: Face Disappointment

Have you ever been disappointed by God? Have you ever come to God with a prayer request only to feel like He either can't hear you or doesn't care?

Be honest, and describe your disappointments in your journal.

Reset 7: Receive and Celebrate Your Forgiveness

Reset Exercise: Wash Away Your "Should"

Whenever you shower, take a few minutes to stand under the water as it pours over you. Bring to mind the specific things that make you feel condemned or guilty. For instance, there is a Pharisee in my mind who regularly likes to accuse and condemn me for things I've said or done in the past. I have to remind myself in those moments of the truth that God has forgiven and forgotten the old sins I've confessed. I let the water wash away the condemning voice and instead focus on my freedom.

As another example, I sometimes struggle with self-hatred. I think, *I should be a better person; I should serve more, give more, be kinder, etc.* As I stand under the shower, I let the water cleanse all the "should" in my life away!

What sins or "should" do you need to let go of?

Once you have them clearly in mind, recite this prayer, or one like it in your own words:

Father, as I place myself beneath the cleansing power of this water, I thank You for placing me under the forgiving power of Your love and grace. I receive Your eternal forgiveness.

Reset 8: Practice a Forgiving Attitude Toward Others

Reset Exercise: Face Judgment of Others

Please open your journal again and write down whom you've judged in the past twenty-four hours. Even if you don't know their name(s), you can write something like, "The moron who kept me waiting at the green arrow in traffic!" Be honest, and take your time.

Reset Exercise: Receive Forgiveness to Give Forgiveness

Find a quiet space where no one will interrupt you. Fill a bowl or basin with water. Sit in a chair, and place your feet in the water. Read John 13:1–34 with your feet in the water. Now close your eyes and imagine Jesus is there, kneeling before you and pouring water over your feet. Each movement of His hand signifies His love and forgiveness of your sins. Receive His love and forgiveness. Be still and worship Him.

Reset 9: Acknowledge That God Loves You Unconditionally, No Matter What

Reset Exercise: How Do You See Yourself?

I have a little exercise I want you to do, but first, carefully read the instructions.

You're going to write down a very simple phrase in your journal and then complete a statement. It is very important that you are raw and honest. Don't write down what you *think* you should write. Instead, finish the statement based on how you really feel about yourself at this moment.

Here you go. Write down and complete this phrase:

Right now, I see myself as _____.

How do you feel about what you wrote?

Reset 10: Know That You Are Created in the Image of God

Reset Exercise: Find Your Center

Let's begin exploring what it means to be created in God's image. The Lutheran theologian and martyr Dietrich Bonhoeffer tried to answer the question this way: "As the image of God, man draws his life entirely from his origin in God..."[1]

What does that mean? Get your journal and whatever you want to use to sketch with, and write the name of God in large block letters, like this:

Inside the O, draw your version of Adam and Eve. Anyone who knows me knows that although I'm a wannabe artist, my talent seems to have peaked at stick figures. If you can do better, go for it!

Are you finished?

What is your rendering of Adam and Eve in the O of God supposed to mean? In this exercise, the O stands for "origin." According to lexico.com, *origin* is defined as "the point or place where something begins, arises, or is derived." In other words, human beings were created by God, from God, and for God. In

---

1. Bonhoeffer, *The Cost of Discipleship*, 22.

God, one is able to truly know Him. It is also in God that a person can really know themselves, others, and the totality of God's creation.

Next, I want you to add four arrows outward from the O, pointing in four different directions, to symbolize the first couple's knowledge of everything emanating from God as their center.

How's your brain doing? Are you beginning to see things a bit differently?

Reset 11: Regain Your Stolen Identity

Reset Exercise: Recognize the Origin of Your Stolen Identity

Please write the name of God again in large block letters in your journal, but this time don't draw the first couple in the O of God. Instead, draw an arrow from the O of God to the outside. Draw the first couple standing *outside* God.

Now put a circle around Adam and Eve individually. You're going to need enough room so you can draw arrows in four directions from each of the circles:

The individual circles represent their new origin: themselves. The arrows represent the fact that they now view everyone and everything, including good and evil and right and wrong, from within themselves.

If you keep reading in Genesis—and I'd encourage you to read at least through chapter 11—you will see the beginning of the tragic effects of living life outside God, which extend to this very day.

Reset 12: Return to the Oasis of God

Reset Exercise: Return to the Oasis of God: Morning Practice

I invite you to use this Reset exercise as a daily practice in the morning and the evening. Here are the guidelines for creating your oasis and the morning practice.

1. Begin by creating a circle that will become the wilderness you visit each day. I mean this quite literally. People who practice yoga haul their yoga mats to the gym, park, and on planes. Their yoga mat is their protected space where they meditate, stretch, pose, and sweat! You don't need a yoga mat, but you do need a defined space in the form of a circle.

Why a circle? It symbolizes the O of God from our earlier Reset exercise. We've come full circle (pardon the pun), and now, instead of Adam and Eve, I want you to literally put yourself in the O of God. Even if you're not sure you believe in God yet, this exercise will allow you to see and feel what finding your origin in God might be like, and who knows—you may even change your mind.

What I do know is changing the brain involves imagination! When I was struggling as a child, I often used my imagination to escape reality, much like author James Thurber's fictional character Walter Mitty. But instead of using our imagination to escape reality, we're going to use it to enter reality. So, imagine the circle you are creating is the place where you will find your center in God.

The circle needs to be big enough for you to sit, stand, or even lay down in. You can create the boundaries from whatever material you want. You could cut a large piece of fabric or mat in the shape of a circle. If you're outside, you could draw a circle in the sand, or place some stones or sticks in the shape of an O. Whatever you do, make it visible, or it won't be effective.

2. Bring several items into your circle: index cards, a pen, a Bible, a piece of fruit, and your journal. Yes, I did say fruit—as in an apple, an orange, grapes, or any type of edible fruit you enjoy. One piece will do.

I invite you to step into the circle at least once a day, but preferably twice a day for the most benefit. If you practice this exercise twice a day, you will enter the circle in the morning before you begin the day and the evening as you end your day.

Let's try it right now! Make a circle using whatever is at hand to mark at least part of its circumference.

3. Once you're in the circle, the first thing I want you to do is to practice some breathing exercises to get still and focused. One very simple and effective breathing exercise I use is called the 4-7-8 relaxing breath exercise. I use it whenever I feel anxious, and it really is effective. Sit in your circle with your back straight. Place the tip of your tongue just behind your front teeth. You will keep your tongue there during the entire exercise. Now, exhale all the air in your lungs. Now close your mouth and inhale slowly through your nose to a mental count of four. Hold your breath for a mental count of seven. Exhale through your mouth and around your tongue for a count of eight. This is one breath. Do this sequence again three more times for a total of four breaths.

Did you try it? How did it feel? It may take some getting used to. The most important part is that exhaling should take twice as long as inhaling, so don't be as concerned about speed as keeping to the mental 4-7-8 count. With practice, you will learn to slow down your breath. You can do this breathing exercise as many times a day as you feel you need to, but always when you begin and leave your circle.

4. Now, let's do some decluttering! This is the stage in the "wilderness" when everything we depend on for our worth and everything we fear is put away. First, ask God verbally or silently to reveal to you anything or anyone you rely on other than Him to define your sense of worth, value, or identity. Your list may include things like these:

- Career
- Looks
- Grades
- Athletic abilities
- Parenting
- People pleasing
- Money
- Spirituality
- Good works
- Other people's opinions of you (by name)

God may reveal these things and people to you in thoughts or images. As you hear from God and write down what is revealed, place each index card outside the circle with a simple prayer:

"God, I am giving _____ up to You. I will no longer allow it/him/her/them to define who I am or how I feel about myself."

At first, you may be disappointed to see how dependent your identity is on other people or circumstances, but don't worry; over time your identity will become less dependent on external things and you will eventually use fewer cards.

Our wilderness experiences can also be fraught with fear and worries. That has been my case since childhood. I've struggled with all kinds of fears, including the following:

- Being left alone
- Rejection (by God and others)
- Death
- Becoming financially poor
- Embarrassment
- Failure

What or whom are you afraid of? Ask God to reveal people, things, or issues that cause fear in your life. Just as you did with the people and things you use to define your worth, write each item individually on a card, place each card outside of the circle, and pray, "God, I am giving _____ up to You. I will no longer allow it/him/her/them to worry or frighten me."

I want you to focus less on how you feel as you do this exercise and more on just doing it. It has been said that feelings are wonderful servants but terrible masters. We are going to learn how not to let our feelings control our lives anymore! Agreed? You're not feeling it? Good! Just do it.

Congratulations! If you have done the above exercises, you are on the way to finding yourself. As you sit in your circle, everything that has defined your worth and value, and all your worries and fears, is now hopefully outside of you. Don't worry if you feel you have not completely cleaned house. That will come.

For now, where do these disciplines leave you? Look at your position. Where are you? In a circle? Not really. I want you to think of that circle as the O of God. Here are three ways to envision the O of God:

1. Know that you are in the center of God. You are inhabiting Him, and He is inhabiting you. This is an answer to one of Jesus's prayers:

> *"'I am praying not only for these disciples but also for all who will ever believe in me through their message. I pray that they will all be one, just as you and I are one—as you are in me, Father, and I am in you. And may they be in us so that the world will believe you sent me.'"*
> —John 17:23

> *"'When I am raised to life again, you will know that I am in my Father, and you are in me, and I am in you.'"*
> —John 14:20

The back of our home has three large glass doors that face south. On sunny but frigid winter days, I love to sit in my reading chair and soak in the sun. It is so warm, and it helps me overcome the winter blues. A good dose of being in the sunshine does my soul well.

2. Soak in the presence of God by meditating on a few Scriptures. (See dalehummel.com for more Scriptures to use for daily meditation.) If you're in a place where you can read out loud, try speaking these verses so you can better focus your mind on the words and their meaning. Imagine you're practicing the 4-7-8 breathing exercise as you breathe in Scripture: as you read the verse(s), take them into your mind, hold the words there for a moment, and then, as though exhaling, try to feel (yes, feel) the meaning of the words. Try it:

> *"Consider the kind of extravagant love the Father has lavished on us—He calls us children of God! It's true; we are His beloved children. And in the same way the world didn't recognize Him, the world does not recognize us either."*
> —1 John 3:1, The Voice

"My loved ones, we have been adopted into God's family; and we are officially His children now. The full picture of our destiny is not yet clear, but we know this much: when Jesus appears, we will be like Him because we will see Him just as He is."
—1 John 3:2, The Voice, emphasis mine

Do you hear that? The Father loves you extravagantly. You are His beloved child. It doesn't matter if no one else recognizes it; all that matters is that you know it. It's official: the adoption papers are signed by the ink of Christ's blood, proof that He gave up His life for you. Soak in the love of God; ask the Holy Spirit to wash you with this truth until it becomes a reality in you. Use your imagination; remember, it is a powerful tool God has given you.

Maybe, like me, you have used your imagination to escape reality and imagine being what you thought the world wanted you to be before you could feel accepted. No more fantasy! Use your God-given imagination to reset your thinking about yourself. Project the words you just read and thought about onto the screen in your mind. See God loving and accepting you just as you are, in whatever state you are in! In other words, you need to see that God loves you, even in your messiness, brokenness, doubts, and confusion. Even in unbelief!

This is the new reality that you will take with you when you leave the circle and head into your day. But don't leave yet. I want you to take something else with you.

3. Get out your piece of fruit! In Galatians 5, the apostle Paul describes nine facets of love, often referred to as the fruits of the Spirit. Here they are:

"But the Holy Spirit produces this kind of fruit in our lives: love, joy, peace, patience, kindness, goodness, faithfulness, gentleness, and self-control."
—Galatians 5:23

You cannot produce what you do not receive and what you do

not enjoy! I want you to select just one facet (fruit) of love for today and read a verse or two that describes it. I'll select kindness. (Check out dalehummel.com, where I've given you several verses to go along with each fruit.)

"When God our Savior revealed his kindness and love, he saved us, not because of the righteous things we had done, but because of his mercy. He washed away our sins, giving us a new birth and new life through the Holy Spirit. He generously poured out the Spirit upon us through Jesus Christ our Savior. Because of his grace he made us right in his sight and gave us confidence that we will inherit eternal life."
—Titus 3:4–7

What are some ways you have experienced the kindness of God? As you think about it, begin enjoying the fruit you brought with you into the circle. If it's really juicy, let it flow down your chin; enjoy the taste as you think about His kindness.

Here are some ways I've experienced God's kindness:

- Through the sacrifice of Jesus, who gave up His life freely for me
- In the fact that He has never abandoned me, despite all the difficulties I've endured, particularly in my childhood and my teenage years
- In being blessed with an incredible wife, children, and grandchildren
- In being allowed to serve great churches
- In the close friends He has surrounded me with through the years
- Through the blessing of good health
- In being able to come to terms with my struggles in the area of mental health
- In being surrounded with some great mental health professionals who have brought insight and meaning into my life
- In the flavor of chocolate–peanut butter ice cream!

Hey, kindness comes in all flavors!

I could go on, but you get the idea, right? As you finish your list of fruit, keep thinking of all the ways God has been kind to you.

Your circle time is nearly complete. In the resources available to you at dalehummel.com, I've laid out for you a way to listen and talk to God that is much more involved and can be included in your circle time with Him. But for now, complete your circle time with your 4-7-8 breathing exercise for a total of four breaths. As you do, concentrate on who you are in the Imago Dei. Enjoy all the fruit of God's kindness to you.

Reset Exercise: See the Good Fruit in Others

Now that you have received and enjoyed the fruit of kindness for yourself (or any fruit of the Spirit you choose), I want you to discipline your mind to look for ways that God reveals His kindness to you and others. This can be as simple as noticing someone opening the door for another. Look for kindness everywhere you go, and when you see it, celebrate it in your mind. Thank God for the kindness you see. If you see a person expressing kindness, say a silent prayer of blessing on him or her. If it's appropriate, tell that person you saw the act of kindness, and share how it blessed you.

For example, recently, my son-in-law rode his bike up a grueling climb to the top of Haleakala Volcano on the island of Maui. It was a strenuous climb of more than ten thousand feet! As he was nearing the top, his body was exhausted, and he didn't know if he would complete the ride. He prayed to God for help, and as he tells it, he "suddenly felt the push of wind, which seemed to carry me to the top." He finished his climb and collapsed on the ground. An older couple who had driven to the top were standing there and walked over to see if he was all right. He shared with them his achievement and God's goodness. They congratulated him, and the woman said, "You deserve some kind of recognition and award!" So she took off her tree of life necklace and placed it around his neck. It made his day!

Reset Exercise: Bless Others, and Bring Out Their Goodness

Here's the second thing I want you to practice today. Place a wreath of kindness figuratively around as many people as you can today through your own acts of kindness. You can express kindness through silent prayer, a smile, opening a door, an appropriate hug for someone you know, high fives, expressions of appreciation, or whatever you can do. Be sincere but intentional. I'm telling you, behaving this way will reset your mind and turn you into a different person!

Reset Exercise: Evening Practice

At the end of your day, lay out your circle, and enter it before turning in for the night. Do your 4-7-8 breathing for four breaths as you enter. While you're in the O of God, I want you to personalize and answer four questions:

1. *In the course of the day, did I take back anything I threw out of the circle today? For instance, did I allow someone at work or in the family to make me feel bad about myself?* If so, just pick up that index card (or create a new one, if you hadn't already created one) and toss it back out of the circle before you go to bed!
2. *Did I let pride get the best of me today? Did I find myself comparing, being jealous, putting others down, or gossiping?* Toss it out of the circle. You don't need to waste your energy by putting others down to feel better about yourself!
3. *What fears or worries crept back into my mind and tied up my emotions?* Name them, pick up the index cards (or create new ones if needed), and toss them out of the circle.
4. *Is there some sin, guilt, or shame I incurred today?* Confess it to the Creator, and receive His awaiting forgiveness. Toss the guilt, shame, and self-loathing out of the circle.

Use the rest of your circle time to savor the kindness you received, saw, and gave away. Eat another piece of fruit if it helps! Here's the key: end your day by resetting your mind into a positive and peaceful mode. I'll bet you will begin sleeping better and waking up with a more positive spirit, too!

Reset 13: Defeat Your Fears by Calling Their Bluff

Reset Exercise: Call Fear's Bluff

What are one or two fears you have been wrestling with? Go ahead and write them down. After you're done, underneath each fear write a positive statement that embraces the outcome you fear!

Here are two examples:

Fear: My throat has been hurting; do I have throat cancer?
Calling fear's bluff: I probably do have throat cancer and will die tomorrow. Bring it! I might as well eat that half-gallon of ice cream now!

Fear: What if my spouse is having an affair?
Calling fear's bluff: My spouse is probably having an affair, and our marriage is through! What shall I fix for dinner? Is this the night to put the trash out?

Notice in my examples that I add something that mocks the fear or moves me on to what is normal, such as fixing dinner or taking out the trash.

Reset 14: Believe the Spiritual Truth About Yourself

Reset Exercise: Believe You Are Already Perfect in Christ

Before you leave your next circle time with God, think about the fruit you chose to enjoy (see page 95). Let's suppose you chose the fruit of patience. Aren't you brave? This exercise is not about becoming patient, but believing that you already are patient in Christ. Therefore, you're not spiritually starting from where you are presently. You are switching perspectives and looking through the lens of where you are spiritually (seated with Christ in the heavenlies).

Using the 4-7-8 breathing technique I taught you (see page 91), do a cycle of three breaths while focusing on the reality that you are already patient in Christ. Accept this as truth. You are living on a higher plane in Christ. This is your destiny in Christ Jesus, and by faith, you have arrived there.

I want you to engage your wonderful God-given imagination now. This is one of the ways you change your brain. As you've learned in previous chapters, the imagination is powerful. We can raise and lower our blood pressure based on the way we use our imagination. We can convince our brain that a spider is crawling up our leg and actually feel like it's happening, to the point we will reach down to smack it! So take that God-given gift of your imagination and enter what you believe will be your first event of the day.

For example, my first challenge will be traffic! There is a series of at least seven stoplights between my house and work. They are stretched out far enough that I can actually get up to 60 mph between them. But invariably, I never make the green lights! I'll get up to speed and then have to slow down and stop—and often it's because someone ahead of me is going too slow. Wow, I'm feeling angry and impatient just typing this!

So, in my circle time with God, I visualize myself in the car at each of the lights. By faith, I see myself in the future! But instead of feeling angry and impatient, trying to jockey for position, I imagine Christ's Spirit in me. I see His patience in my mind's eye. He is far less concerned about making all the green lights.

He savors the moments to stop. He looks around at those ahead, beside, and behind Him, and He thinks about who they are and what their lives must be like. Because patience is an attribute of love, He uses the time spent at the stoplights to pray for them, bringing them before His Father, asking His Abba to bless them.

Patience is the practice of putting others first, even when it inconveniences us. In Christ, we learn that there's no such thing as inconvenience. Everything is an opportunity.

As fear strikes me with the thought that I'll be late if I don't push the pedal to the floor as though I'm in a Mario Kart video game, I call fear's bluff: "I probably will be late! I may even get fired. Well, then I won't have to worry about any more traffic. Bring it!"

Proceed through the rest of the expected events of your day, as much as time allows.

Reset 15: Identify What You Want in Community with Others
Reset 16: Create the Environment for Genuine Community

Reset Exercise: Hold Your Tongue

In your own circle time with God, make it a daily prayer and a conscious habit to replace every nasty thing you want to tell someone with an opposite word of praise. This forces you to look for the good in them rather than obsessing on the meanness or evil you see in them. What you will soon discover if you do this is that you can actually begin to change their behavior.

An added bonus: You are also resetting your own mind!

Reset Exercise: Form a New Community

Is there someone you know who you think might benefit from

forming a Reset Community with you? Make a potential list right now in your Reset Journal of the people you think could benefit from being in community with you.

If you're so inclined, pray over the list and ask God to help direct you to the people you should ask. Meet one-on-one over coffee and tell the person how this book and its principles and practices are changing your life. When you engage the people on your list, ask them if they would be willing to read the book with you and meet once a week to simply exchange what you're both discovering. As you each read the last chapter on community, ask them if they would like to continue with you in forming a close gathering that meets regularly for friendship, prayer, healing, and hope.

Use the headings of this chapter to serve as a charter for how your Reset Group might function. In other words, aim to be a community where together, you practice exhibiting the following characteristics:

- Genuine
- Joyful
- Loving
- Vulnerable
- Forgiving
- Worshipful

If you are not a person of faith, you can leave "worshipful" as an option. If you are a follower of Christ with a friend you would like to invite into community who may not ascribe to Christianity, that's okay. Give them a copy of the book to read first. You may find that they are willing to be a part of the group, as long as they don't feel pressure to convert! Don't try to convert them; let them simply experience God working in and through them and let them decide with God's help. Focus your attention on learning to love them unconditionally, as God does each one of us.

As you describe the aim of your Reset Community, agree to the seven attitudes that Dietrich Bonhoeffer described as ministries within the community:

- The ministry of holding one's tongue
- The ministry of meekness
- The ministry of listening
- The ministry of helpfulness
- The ministry of bearing
- The ministry of proclaiming
- The ministry of thankfulness

My suggestion is, when two or more of you agree on what you want your Reset Community to become, also agree on the seven attitudes you will seek to practice. I believe the next steps would be to use the chapters of this book as a basis for your discussions. Before doing so, have each person agree to the following guidelines:

1. I/we agree to review the aim and attitudes of our Reset Group at the beginning of each meeting.
2. I/we agree to ask the group members if they feel we are making progress in living out the aim and attitudes of our Reset Group.
3. I/we agree to respect each other's information and keep what is shared in the group in the strictest confidentiality.
4. I/we agree to attend every session, barring any emergencies.
5. I/we agree that our purpose is not to fix each other but to listen, encourage, and help only when members of the group ask for it.

Here's a suggested format you may want to follow. It is important that you do not hurry through this. Feel free to adjust the sessions to fit your needs as a group.

Week 1: Briefly discuss my story and how you can relate to it. Take the time to talk about your own story. I suggest you limit each person's time of sharing to no more than ten minutes. It is important that each group member shares his or her story.

Week 2: Discuss what you learned about the mind and the brain. How has the human condition of sin affected your mindset?

Week 3: Discuss how neuroplasticity can reset your thinking. Include discussion on the importance of thoughts, images, and ideas.

Week 4: Discuss chapter 3 of the book.

Weeks 5 and 6: Discuss chapter 4.

Week 7: Discuss chapter 5.

Week 8: Discuss chapter 6.

Week 9: Discuss chapter 7.

You can find many resources to supplement your group meetings at dalehummel.com, including specific resources for each chapter, as well as a Reset course video in which I teach each chapter of the book to a group and leave time for group discussion.

Acknowledgments

This book would not be possible if it were not for some very amazing people that God placed in my life.

I am thankful for Jacqueline, whom God used to help me discover and heal the little boy in me who had been left behind. To Brad, thank you for pointing out that my "crazy" thoughts had a name—OCD! Thanks for showing me how to manage it. Dr. Sood, you have taught me so much about the brain and how to change the way I think.

Ben, Bethany and Tim, thanks for loving your dad even when he seemed distant.

I want to acknowledge my closest friends and family who have prayed and always been there for me.

Thank you to my writing coach Amanda Rooker of Split Seed Media. You were a wonderful teacher. Thanks to Sarah Hage for reading through the manuscript many times and making edits and suggestions. Thanks to Greg Johnson my agent who patiently pursued publishers because he believed others could be helped by my story. Finally, thank you Robert Walker of Core Media Group for taking the risk and publishing this book!

About the Author

Dale Hummel is the Senior Pastor of Wooddale Church in Eden Prairie Minnesota, where he leads a multi-site congregation of five thousand attendees. His passion is to spread the hope of the gospel, "here, near and far." In *Reset: Live Every Day Like It's a New Day*, Dale shares how he found transforming hope despite chronic childhood abuse and living with the challenges of a mental illness called OCD. In this very practical book, Dale uses his gift of teaching to show the reader how they too can overcome the past to find lasting hope and freedom. To learn more about Reset, or to invite Dale to come and speak at your event please see Dalehummel.com